Table of Contents

List of Figures

List of Tables

E^2 Cargo Transport--The Necessary Inclusion of Primary Oceanic Airlift

I. Introduction

General Issue

The United States Air Force spends approximately $8B in aviation fuel every year, with Mobility Air Forces consuming 50% of the fuel used on an annual basis (Maybury, 2012:7). For the Mobility Air Forces a majority of the cargo movements occur over non-threatening territories or waters. One such example is the movement of palletized cargo across the two primary oceans, the Atlantic Ocean and the Pacific Ocean. Over approximately the last 12 years the primary routes have been eastward from the United States with aircraft transiting the Atlantic Ocean on a near-continuous basis.

Background and Motivation

Every action taken by our United States Air Force comes at a fiscal price with an assumed checks and balances in the system to make sure we are accomplishing our process in the most efficient way possible. In the title, E^2 means combining and considering both efficiency and effectiveness in every decision that we make as stewards of our nation's financial resources. Our nation and the lives of those dedicated to our nation's protection expect a more successful, maneuverable and positioned Air Force as time progresses. The Air Force as a community is short-sighted to think that only one (efficiency or effectiveness) is important at a time, in fact, they both play a huge part in our success. Often we fail to consider history in how we acquire our aircraft. We learned this in developing the C-17 and the AMST and hopefully will take our lessons forward in purchasing the KC-46A. This may allow the Air Force as a culture to seek an efficient and effective relationship, thus exponentially building the required flexibility of a lean fighting force.

The United States most modern strategic airlift aircraft is the C-17A Globemaster III (Knight, 2008:10). This aircraft is a very important force multiplier and a key to the Rapid Mobility process for any war effort or disaster response. The aircraft has been pivotal in the success of Operation IRAQI FREEDOM, Operation ENDURING FREEDOM and several smaller operations. The C-17A is an excellent airlifter; however it is a niche aircraft. The C-17A was designed to carry out-sized and oversized cargo, including tanks, helicopters and missile launchers (Knight, 2008:10). Our entire Air Force is made up of niche aircraft; some have a bigger niche than other aircraft. As an example the C-17A was designed around carrying the M-1 tank for the Army, but it has expanded into several other arenas with a plethora of missions (Kennedy, 2004:32). However, with the ongoing wars, some C-17A aircraft are nearing or have exceeded their planned proposed lifespan of 30,000 hours or 30 years (Robertson, 2013:email) . A large portion of flying hours is spent "crossing the pond"; in other words, flying across the ocean. The motivation of this research is not to buy another airplane for the Air Force, but to put some efficiency in the transoceanic cargo movement process that will in the long run increase the effectiveness of our Air Force as a whole.

Problem Statement

The problem statement is simple: The United States Air Force is wasting an extraordinary amount of money fueling oceanic airlift and at the same time are quickly diminishing the life expectancy of our primary strategic airlifters, specifically the C-17A. The Air Force needs to devise a solution to bring down the cost per pound of cargo in fuel expenditure for organic palletized lift.

Research Objectives/Questions/Hypotheses

The objective of this research is to determine if there is a better, less-expensive, but just as effective option to move 463L pallets across the ocean instead of using the costly C-17A. Fuel cost is the primary variable of interest for this evaluation. It may be determined that at the current price point for fuel, the purchase and change to a Boeing 777 Freighter would not make fiscal sense. The real question is then:

1. At what fuel price point would it make sense to actually purchase and operate the new oceanic airlift aircraft?
2. Which aircraft is more efficient in carrying palletized cargo?
3. Which aircraft is more effective in carrying palletized cargo?
4. Will the inclusion of this new oceanic airlift aircraft reduce or minimize the need for costly C-17 overhauls or extended depots?
5. Can the purchase of a Boeing 777F be funded with fuel savings?

Research Focus

The focus of this research project is to determine if there is a better, more effective, efficient, and overall less expensive option to oceanic airlift than the C-17A. Cost data is analyzed to make this proposal and possibly market this idea to senior Air Force leadership. The research also examined different price points for fuel to determine at what point is purchasing/operating the Boeing 777 Freighter economical for oceanic palletized cargo airlift.

Methodology

The most difficult part of this research is determining a baseline for comparison in cost for cargo capability. Total cost per flight hour is a nebulous idea. There are several costs that contribute to the actual cost of flying an aircraft each hour. This actual cost is very hard to define for the Air Force. As an example, pilots are required to fly an aircraft. For the airlines, it is simple, they hire a pilot to do the job of a pilot and that alone; the Air Force is a different story. A pilot in the Air Force is hired first as an officer, then a pilot. In addition, there are several support functions that contribute to the flying mission that are difficult to quantify monetarily. In addition, actual operation costs for the Boeing 777 Freighter are not possible to obtain as that data is proprietary for those companies operating the aircraft. Thus, a very tangible and real aspect of the cost of flying was chosen to be evaluated: fuel burn, the fuel burned to accomplish the mission, from engine start at origin to engine shutdown at destination.

Assumptions/Limitations

There are several assumptions that must be considered throughout this research project. Many of the assumptions may seem common sense, the remaining are assumptions that are needed in order to keep this research at a reasonable scale. The first assumption is that the Air Force is willing to spend money on new airplanes in order to potentially save money in the long run. The second assumption is that if the airport is currently able to support a Boeing 747, DC-10 or C-5, then it has the structure in place to support a Boeing 777F. The third assumption is that the C-17 is utilized for oversized and outsized oceanic cargo airlift. The fourth assumption is the Boeing 777F can carry

4

463L pallets. The last assumption is that the Boeing 777F can cross the ocean without being air refueled and each pallet position is maximized with its weight potential. The maximum weight potential is the maximum allowable cargo weight for that chosen route.

The most difficult limitation encountered is availability of data for the Boeing 777F. Some of the required information could be proprietary or limited release. Those issues are dealt with sensitivity and err on the side of caution.

Implications

The results of this study are not necessarily to up-end the usage of the C-17A by the United States Air Force, but to approach its usage in a more common sense and responsible way. Current economic restrictions make it imperative that we utilize our resources in a responsible manner that ensures current fiscal responsibility to both the United States and the USAF. At the same time, the USAF requires the capability of the C-17A for years to come without "flying the wings" off the jet by utilizing the aircraft inappropriately in environments that don't require its capabilities. Again, the purpose of this paper to institute a change in culture; the Air Force and a Department of Defense must evaluate operations in both an efficient and an effective light to ensure future capabilities for the United States.

II. Literature Review

"To improve is to change; to be perfect is to change often."

Winston Churchill

To be in control of something you must truly understand it. The United States Government and the United States Air Force are always seeking for operational control. However, a majority of the time the USAF seeks only to evaluate itself based on the instantaneous results. For example, a pallet of cargo reached its destination in 2 days. This could be considered a job "well done". However, what other operations were impacted by this accomplishment—was the instantaneous result at the expense of ensuring future capabilities? This literature review walks the reader through the history of airlift; the current requirements for airlift; the history of the C-17A; the history of the Boeing 777F, a comparison of the C-17A and the Boeing 777F; the current overfly status of the C-17A; and, the energy future of the Air Force. By the end of the literature review, the reader will understand the history of the aircraft, the USAF's current energy challenges and why every action to find solutions to increase both our efficiency and effectiveness, E^2 is required.

History of Airlift

In retrospect, the need for airlift has been quite small until recent history. Today in 2013, airlift aircraft have not been used by the military for even a hundred years; "as early as World War I, the Army used airplanes to transport cargo and personnel" (Battershell, 1999:8). However, cargo movement has often been an after-thought or an event that was assumed to occur. In the late 1920's the Douglas Company constructed the first dedicated cargo aircraft, the C-1 (Figure 1).

Prior to the development of this aircraft, cargo was often moved for the Army by the bomber aircraft (Battershell, 1999:8). Fortunately, the United States has not had to fight a recent war on its own soil, but this has predecated the need for a large airlift fleet. According to Major General Robert M. Webster, Commander of the Air Transport Command in 1947, he stated:

> I feel that we have come out of that war (World War II) with an additional type, the transport plane, and that we should think in terms of bomber-fighter-transport—since they are all equally important—and they must be properly balanced to each other if we are to be prepared to conduct successful operations. (Battershell, 1999:8)

Successful missions that closely followed this speech helped define a major role of United States Transportation Command and Air Mobility Command.

A major event defining the future of airlift occurred in 1948. This event was the Berlin Airlift.

At midnight on 23 June, the Russians ordered the cutting of the grid carrying electricity supplies from the central electricity generator in their sector to the Western Sectors of Berlin, and at six o'clock the next morning they also severed all road and barge traffic to and from the city, at the same time halting all supplies—including coal, food and fresh milk—which were drawn from the Soviet Sector...There was no longer any doubt: Berlin was under seige. (Jackson, 1988:42)

Although initially many considered that this could turn into a combat event, this purely ended up being a air transport event. The Americans and British had the aircraft that were capapble for doing the airlift. The results of the airlift were astounding (Figure 2):

Monthly tonnages

Month	US		British		Total	
	Flights	Tonnages	Flights	Tonnages	Flights	Tonnages
26 June – 31 July 1948	8,117	41,188	5,919	29,053	14,036	70,241
August	9,796	73,632	8,252	45,002	18,048	118,634
September	12,905	101,871	6,682	36,556	19,587	138,427
October	12,139	115,793	5,943	31,245	18,082	147,038
November	9,046	87,963	4,305	24,629	13,351	112,592
December	11,655	114,572	4,834	26,884	16,489	141,456
January	14,089	139,223	5,396	32,739	19,485	171,962
February	12,051	120,404	5,043	31,846	17,094	152,250
March	15,530	154,480	6,627	41,686	22,157	196,166
April	19,129	189,972	6,896	45,405	26,025	235,377
May	19,365	192,247	8,352	58,547	27,717	250,794
June	18,451	182,722	8,049	57,602	26,545	240,324

Figure 2: Monthly tonnages for Berlin Airlift (Jackson, 1988:146)

The airlift, initially intended to support the military troops within the city, eventually swelled up in to a mission supporting the entire western sector of the city of Berlin. This airlift was completed at any cost, the goal was effectiveness. As with infancy stages of any program or mission, there are always mistakes. Unfortunately, in the case of this airlift mission, there were both aircraft accidents on the ground, in the air and the accompanying casualties. The costs of the Berlin Airlift in regards to fuel equated to more than 100,000,000 gallons of aviation fuel (Pearcy, 1997:103). This mission was a "no-fail" mission and it was accomplished in that manner. In this case effectiveness was the primary goal—it was a no-fail mission at a cost of both lives and aircraft.

As with all airlift movements, fuel is a necessity. In the case of the Berlin Airlift it was no different. Although fuel was not a primary expense in missions as it is today. Although expensive, the benefits of airlift continued to outweigh the costs.

The Berlin Airlift set the stage for a no-fail effective mission. Major events form and shape businesses and militaries for the future. The Berlin Airlift was no different. Following the Berlin Airlft, the needs of airlift were futher defined. The delination between strategic and tactical airlift was further defined.

Airlift, although simple in concept is actually very diverse in reality. When discussing airlift, there are two different types of airlift: strategic and tactical. First, according the Congressional Budget Office (CBO), in a paper written on the C-17A, "Airlift aircraft provide the United States with a capability to rapidly deliver, reinforce, and sustain combat forces worldwide" (CBO, 1993:2). According to the *Air Force Basic Doctrine, Organization and Command*, Airlift is:

> …operations to transport and deliver forces and materiel through the air in support of strategic, operational, or tactical objectives" (AFDD 3-17, *Air Mobility Operations*). The rapid and flexible options afforded by airlift allow military forces and national leaders the ability to respond and operate in a variety of situations and time frames. The global reach capability of airlift provides the ability to apply US power worldwide by delivering forces to crisis locations. It serves as a US presence that demonstrates resolve and compassion in humanitarian crisis. (LeMay Center, 2011:51)

9

Strategic and tactical airlift differ primarily by the locations they are responsible for moving cargo. Often airlift aircraft are separated out depending on the role they will play.

The two different airlift roles discussed in the halls of the Pentagon are "strategic" and "tactical" airlift. As an example, the C-141 was a strategic airlift aircraft, so its primary role was strategic airlift. However, according to the Air Force, the term stragegic airlift and tactical airlift do not exist in their doctrine. In the *Air Force Doctrine Document 3-17, Air Mobility Operations*, a definition of strategic or tactical airlift cannot be found. However, similar terms can be found. According to doctrine, strategic airlift is considered intertheater airlift. Intertheater airlift is defined as

> The common-user airlift linking theaters to the continental United States and to other theaters as well as the airlift within the continental United States... intertheater airlift is normally conducted by the heavy, longer range, intercontinental airlift assets but may be augmented with shorter range aircraft when required (LeMay Center, 2006:107).

Likewise, tactical airlift is not defined in Air Force Doctrine. However, intratheater airlift is defined. Again, according to *Air Force Doctrine Document 3-17, Air Mobility Operations,*

> intratheater airlift is airlift conducted within a theater. Assets assigned to a geographic combatant commander or attached to a subordinate joint force commander normally conduct intratheater airlift operations. Intratheater airlift provides air movement and delivery of personnel and equipment directly into objective areas through air landing, airdrop, extraction, or other delivery techniques as well as the air logistic support of all theater forces, including those engaged in combat operations, to meet specific theater objectives and requirements. (LeMay Center, 2006:107)

As intertheater and intratheater airlift were further defined with historical assistance of events like the Berlin Airlift, more aircraft were developed to meet the current and future needs of the Air Force and the nation. Not only has history help shaped the airlift force, but so have force structure studies.

Mobility Capabilities and Requirements Study-2016

Planned and unplanned events shape the structure and the capabilities that a military force brings to the fight. The world and thus the national threats within the world have been continuously changing. According to the *Mobility Capabilities and Requirements Study-2016 (MCRS-16) Executive Summary*,

> In addition to the refinement of U.S. strategic priorities, important fact-of-life changes have occurred since the MCS was completed that place new demands on the mobility system. These changes include a higher level of engagement around the world, increased reliance on the Reserve Components, increased reliance on airlift to move equipment and supplies that were once moved almost exclusively via surface transport, the introduction of new specialized equipment (e.g., Mine Resistant Ambush Protected vehicles), the continued growth of Special Operations Forces, the establishment of United States Africa Command, and the increase in Army and Marine Corps end strength. (Office of the Secretary of Defense, 2010:1)

Changes like these discussed above are what drive the requirements that the United States Air Force must be ready to respond to and support. The three cases for the MCRS-16 are displayed in Figure 3, note the high requirements for inter and intratheater airlift.

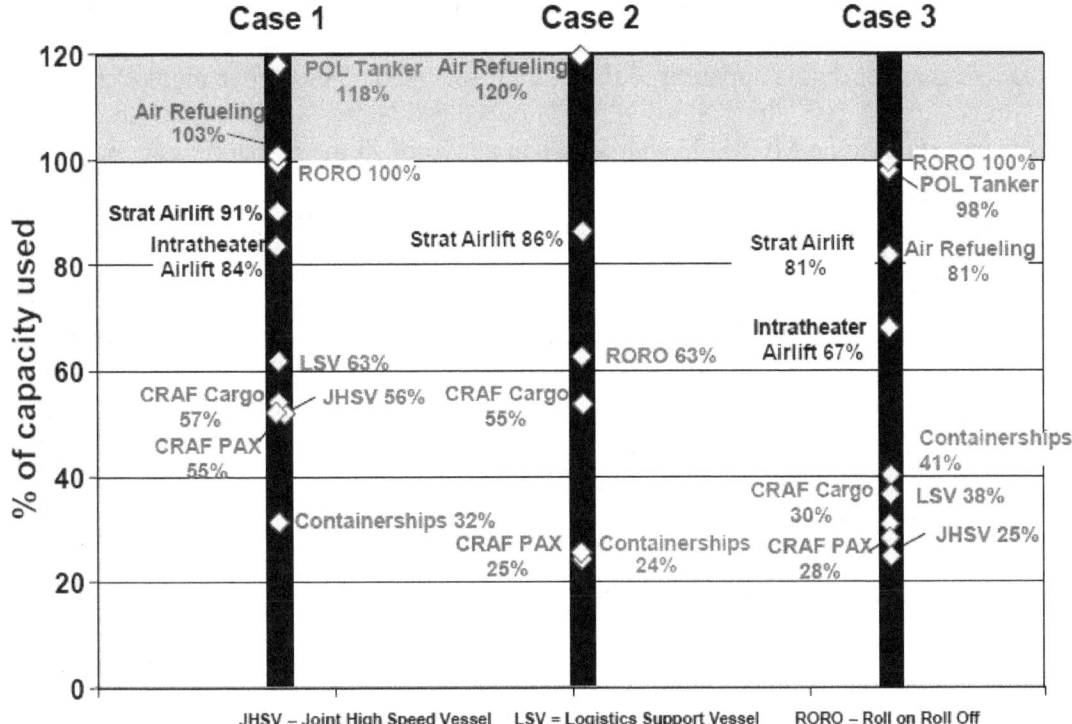

Figure 3: Mobility System Utilization by MCRS Case

(Department of Defense, 2010:5)

There are several critics of the MCRS-16, especially the Government

Accountability Office (GAO). First, it is important to understand the perspective of the

GAO when evaluating the MCRS-16. According to the GAO, "the intent of the MCRS-

16 was to provide senior leaders with a detailed understanding of the range of mobility

capabilities needed for possible future strategic environments and help them make

investment decisions regarding mobility systems" (GAO, 2010:1). The possibility exists

to understand both point of views, the GAO and the Department of Defense. First, the

Department of Defense is charged with ensuring the capabilities exist in order to execute

the military arm of our government, in an ever changing environment where data is

instantly available by one avenue or another on the internet. Similarily, the GAO is charged with ensuring the different arms of the United States Government operate in a responsible manner that is apparent to the common citizen. The Department of Defense does clearly state in the MCRS-16 that they can accomplish the missions as conducted by their analysis. According to the executive summary of the MCRS-16,

> The capacity of the Department's strategic airlift fleet exceeds the peak demand in each of the three MCRS cases. The programmed strategic airlift fleet, which consists of 223 C-17s and 111 C-5s, provides a capacity of 35.9 million ton-miles per day (MTM/D). The peak for MCRS Case 1, which represents the highest level of modeled strategic airlift demand, required 32.7 MTM/D. Case 2 required 30.7 MTM/D, and Case 3 required 29.1 MTM/D. (Office of the Secretary of Defense, 2010:4)

The programmed strategic airlift fleet, is a very capable fleet, but it is important to note the Civil Reserve Air Fleet (CRAF). The strategic airlift capability of the United States is only as capable as our CRAF.

CRAF in terms of mobility are broken into two categories (Figure 3), either CRAF passenger or CRAF cargo. Important to note, is that the primary aircraft for moving passengers and cargo are the Boeing 767/777 and the Boeing 747, respectively. These aircraft have much more capability both in regards to passengers and cargo than any of our mobility aircraft, except the C-5 in regards to cargo. Additionally, all of the CRAF aircraft can be considered strategic airlift aircraft. Although in the MCRS-16, the CRAF plays a lesser role, in regards to percentage, it is arguable that they play a larger role than given credit.

The Department of Defense relies on CRAF as the "primary means of delivering passengers and bulk air cargo. Projected CRAF cargo capacity is significant, and greatly exceeds the requirements for all MCRS cases" (Department of Defense, 2010:6). In the

MCRS-16 study the CRAF requirements paled in comparison to the requirement. Another important and critical part of the airlift structure is the C-17A.

History of the C-17A

This history of the C-17A is long and varied. The concept of the C-17A "began in the early 1970's as the Advanced Medium Short Range Take Off and Landing (AMST)—a prototype for a tactical cargo airlifter" (Battershell, 1999:3). During the early 1970's, the Air Force was seeking an upgrade to the tactical airlift fleet that had been utilized extensively in the Vietnam War (Battershell, 1999:3). Significant to note that the aircraft was intended as a tactical aircraft, not one for strategic purposes—this battle between tactical and strategic, significantly impacted the aircraft and the timeline for development.

In the early 1970's, McDonnel Douglas and Boeing both built and tested aircraft in competition for the AMST contract. During this timeframe, David Packard, Deputy Secretary of Defense, believed that "prototyping, which tested and evaluated competing prototypes before awarding the production contract, would hold down development costs" (Kennedy, 2004:7). In the first two years of funding, the program received $6 million (FY1972) and $25 million (FY1973), but then "in December 1973, the House Appropriations Committee decreased the authorization for fiscal year 1974 from $65 to $25 million" (Kennedy, 2004:9). This put a major damper on the goal of declaring the AMST initial operating capability (IOC) in the mid-1970's (Kennedy, 2004:9). In addition to funding from the government, both Boeing and McDonnell Douglas invested their own money towards the AMST venture, believing that "commercial airlines and foreign countries would purchase the aircraft as well" (Kennedy, 2004:9). During the 1970's there was continuous banter within Congress among the different committees in determing the airlift requirements for the United States military. In addition to the unstable requirements, politics also played a significant role in the acquisition process.

In 1975, as a result of the Vietnam war, all tactical airlift was transferred over to the Military Airlift Command; this transition included the AMST program (Kennedy, 2004:10). The command further defined some of the requirements for this AMST aircraft: "reduced the long range cruising speed to .68 Mach at 30,000 feet and above; changed the STOL (Short-TakeOff-Landing) payload from 28,000 pounds (500 nautical mile combat radius) to 27,000 pounds (400 mile combat radius); and increased the conventional theater payload from 58,000 pounds to 62,000 pounds (1,000 nautical miles), which accomodated the weight growth of the self-propelled howitzer" (Kennedy, 2004:10). McDonnell Douglas responded to the Military Airlift Commands requirements with the YC-15 and Boeing built the YC-14 (Figures 4-6).

Figure 6: McDonnell Douglas YC-15 (Kennedy, 2004:196)

By the end of testing, and evolving requriements, the YC-15 had demonstrated air refueling, STOL with a glide slope of nearly six degrees and no flare and the YC-14 had accomplished load tests of the howitzer, the AN-1G attack helicopter, ground loading of the Army's M60A tank, to name a few (Kennedy, 2004:12). Major General Howard W. Leaf, commander of the Air Force Test and Evaluation Command, expressed satisfaction with both the YC-15 and YC-14, with a source selection in 1977 and production beginning in 1978 (Kennedy, 2004:12). Just as the plan was about to come to fruition, the Department of Defense landscape changed again.

The Arab-Israeli Yom Kippur War analysis redesignated the need for the type of airlift required for the United States Department of Defense. "Hampered by the vast distances (on average 6,450 miles one way), unavailability of en route facilities, and lack of an air refueling capability, the crisis pressed US strategic airlift resource..." (Kennedy,

2004:12). This combined with indications from war plans that strategic airlift was still in a shortage, led to more strategic airlift, not just the tactical airlift cure found in the AMST program (Kennedy, 2004:12). Strategic changes, combined with more political strife, further endangered the AMST program.

Political dancing continued. In March of 1976, the Senate Armed Services' Research and Development Subcommittee provided the Military Airlift Command with another roadblock: it was indicated that "the Air Force had not properly justified the AMST and recommended against funding full-scale engineering development;" further more, the acting chariman, Patrick J. Leahy (D-VT) stated, "it would seem essential that the principal user (the Army) of an aircraft should have a major role in determining if a requirement existed and if so, what requirement" (Kennedy, 2004:14). As a result of the studies accomplished after the Yom Kippur War, the Air Staff got further involved in the aircraft development process. At the forefront of the Air Staff's thinking was the requirement for strategic airlift. In March of 1976, the Air Staff queried Military Airlift Command and Air Force Systems Command as follows:

> Could non-STOL deriviatives of one or both of the AMST prototype designs be developed to meet the following intertheater airlift missions? (1) Transport without refueling any single type of equipment presently carried by the C-5 over the current unrefueled C-5 range at maximum payload. (2) Transport on a routine basis an M-60 tank weighing 111,000 lbs over the following unrefueled ranges: (A) 4000 NM, (B) 3000 NM, (C) 2000 NM. (Kennedy, 2004:15)

It was determined that a strategic derivative of the tactical AMST could not be developed without major engineering changes in the design. These major engineering changes included a "larger cargo box, new wings and more powerful engines (Kennedy, 2004:15).

However, this did not preclude the production of the AMST, but further deterioration of the strategic airlift capability in the United States did.

The Military Airlift Command had not given up on the AMST, but it was acknowledged that the plane must have some sort of strategic capability. This capability was vaguely defined by Lieutenant General Alton D. Slay of Air Force Research and Development when he stated "to avoid degrading the acknowledged strategic shortfall, the AMST must be able to transport a meaningful self-support payload to the theater of operations…" (Kennedy, 2004:15). Further need for strategic and tactical airlift resulted from two late-coming events: the release of an 18-month Army study and C-5 wing issues. In 1977, the Army released a study of tactical airlift requirements, stating that a "tank-carrying AMST offered the Army the 'most flexible and efficient tactical airlift system'" (Kennedy, 2004:16). Furthering the need for airlift, it was discovered that the C-5 had major wingbox issues. The Office of the Secretary of Defense determined the C-5 fleet should be reduced, driving the fleet from 120 to 81 aircraft, without coordinating with the Army (Kennedy, 2004:16). This left the Army in a very tough position, because not only was the Air Force unable to meet their current needs, but the AMST program failed to be funded as President Carter took over the White House. "By the end of October 1979, the matter was over; Defense Secretary Harold Brown had decided to improve the strategic airlift capability. He had met with Air Force Chief of Staff Lew Allen and advised him to cease associated activities on the AMST program and proceed with the C-X program, emphasizing strategic airlift as the primary mission, an outsize cargo capability, and a fiscal year 1987 initial operational date" (Kennedy,

2004:20). The C-X had just over 7 years to be IOC, a challenge the AMST could not even meet.

The new C-X will be a strategic airlifter. Defense Secretary Harold Brown commented saying that "the aircraft will be optimized for intertheater, not intratheater missions" (Kennedy, 2004:23). This statement was followed up with a team established to put together the requirements of this new C-X airaft. This team was named the C-X Task Force and was comprised of five C-130 pilots with Vietnam combat experience, a C-5 pilot, a C-141 pilot and a helicopter pilot (Kennedy, 2004:25). With the team built with a plethora of C-130 experienced pilots, it is not surprising that the C-17A ended up being a very tactical aircraft, as ananylsis for the C-X closely mirrored that of the AMST program. The Air Force treated the C-X just as they did the AMST applying the following concept, "This is what the Air Force wants the plane to do. You design it to accomplish the tasks" (Kennedy, 2004:28). This process is reverse of the normal acquisition process as the C-X was already approved by Congress, now the requirements were being built. This allowed for "the sky to be the limit" on what the team wanted the aircraft to be able to accomplish. An example of this approach is founded during the analysis of the aircraft requirements.

The C-X Task Force spent a large amount of time analyzing airfields throughout the world to determine the capablilites required of the C-X. "Through airfield analysis the task force looked to one airplane to perform both airlift missions: strategic and tactical" (Kennedy, 2004:29). Figure 7 shows the number of airfields evaluated and how many more airfields were available, once you reached the 3,000 foot length of airfields. This requirement is very similar to that of the tactical aircraft, the AMST, not the intended strategic airlift aircraft, the C-X, reference the inter-theater airlift definition at the beginning of the paper.

C-X Task Force Analysis on Number of Available Airfields

Runway Length x Width	Africa	Central Europe	South America	Middle East	Free World Minus US
>5,000' x >150'	127	50	144	133	847
>5,000' x >90'	686	254	520	400	3,645
>4,000' x >90'	1,125	305	1,149	536	5,938
>3,000' x >90'	1,900	446	2,759	681	10,083
>2,000' x >90'	2,969	740	5,057	747	16,192

Figure 7: C-X Airfield Analysis (Kennedy, 2004:29)

Clearly, the task force, and the Air Force, had no intention of just settling for a strategic-airlift-only aircraft. They spent the time and energy to evaluate over 16,000 airfields for their tactical airlift capabilities. This airfield data later found itself in the preliminary system operational concept (PSOC).

The PSOC was issued on 22 January 1980 and stated the following requirements, many of them being tactical:

> The C-X force must be an effective carrier of outsize cargo, as well as other categories, in the intertheater (long range) and intratheater (austere environment) airlift mission areas. Accordingly, a basic C-X mission will airlift outsize/oversize heavy firepower/equipment from CONUS/overseas locations over long distances (with air refueling, if required) directly into small austere airfields close to the battle area, offload and recover to a theater MOB. When time urgent movement to battle areas via ground Lines of Communication (LOCs) is constrained by an inadequate road/rail system or enemy action, a portion of the C-X force will shuttle outsize firepower and other cargo forward to small, austere airfields before reverting to the inter-theater mode. It is precisely this combination of outsize, long range, and intra-theater airland performance that is essential to capitalize upon the characteristics of the existing airlift system and signicantly expand its ability to rapidly close/resupply or reinforce a modern US combat force anywhere in the world. This is primary in design and employment

of the C-X force as an intergral part of the total airlift system. (Kennedy, 2004:30-31)

The initial performance criteria for the C-X listed in the PSOC are stated as the following:

> The PSOC defined performance criteria are airlifting a maximum of 130,000 pounds (three infantry fighting vehicles or one combat configured M-60 or XM-1 tank at 2.25Gs) and landing on a 3,000-foot-long runway or less, using maximum braking and idle reverse and carrying a payload of at least 100,000 pounds. The austere runway would be either paved or unpaved with an unpaved surface rates at CBR 9 and able to sustain 100 passes. The aircraft would have an unrefueled range of at least 2,800 nautical miles carrying a payload of no less than 100,000 pounds or 75 percent of the maximum aircraft cabin load at 2.25Gs. The C-X would also be capable of backing up a 3 percent grade with a 130,000 pound payload, making a 180-degree turn on a 90-foot-wide runway, operating from a 60-foot-wide runway with turnaround areas, and performing airdrop requirements. The aircraft would be able to operate in a "modestly hostile" environment. The personnel airdrop goal was for at least 100 combat-equipped paratroopers exiting the aircraft plus four standard equipment bundles in 55 seconds as well as the airdrop/extraction of vehicles weighing up to 50,000 pounds. The minimum acceptable long-range cruise airspeed was .70 Mach. The C-X would have a peacetime utilization rate of 2.5-3.5 hours per day—up to 10.0 hours per day during sustained wartime operations with a surge capability of 12.5 hours for up to 45 days. (Kennedy, 2004:32)

It is intersting to note that very few of the requirements, if any were really built for a strategic airlifter. It seems as if the aircraft was built as a tactical aircraft with a hint of strategic airlift. A significant part of this program to remember is that the aircraft was approved before the specifications were put forth, and the requirements were not yet established. This uncertainty of design, although partially explained in the PSOC, were yet to be set in stone; instead they were written in sand on a stormy beach.

The original plan of the C-X was for it to be a pure strategic airlift aircraft. However, the Secretary of the Air Force was eventually swayed. After seeing several years of the C-5 not being able to land at forward austere bases, the Secretary of the Air

Force Hans Mark, realized the C-X needed to be something other than a pure strategic airlift aircraft (Kennedy, 2004:34). This reasoning is more than understandable, the capability was needed to land at austere locations that the C-5 was intended to serve. However, the Air Force now had a politcal mud field to walk through. "Members of Congress voiced criticism and skepticism…Representative Ichord (D-MO) cited the millions of dollars spent on weapon system programs only to end up terminated, singling out the $7 billion for a manned penetrating bomber, $240 million for the AMST, and $350 million for the prototype of the Surface Effects Ship" (Kennedy, 2004:36). The Air Force was not trusted by all members of Congress as stated by Representative Jack Edwards (D-AL):

> …what I am trying to get at is, here you are talking to me and to us about this massive new program for cargo planes when you are not even supporting the primary cargo planes you have. Are we just simply going to start a brand new plane, because that is the thing to do, and then immediately start underfunding it? I would feel a lot happier if you came in here and said we need $511 million to get the C-5 back on track. After you did that, then you came to me and said we need a C-X. It seems like we are always out there flirting with the will o' the wisp for something and we are not doing our homework day after day on keeping these things going. (Kennedy, 2004:37)

The sting of the AMST not even being selected, only prototypes being built, was still felt within Congress, despite efforts to allow the Air Force to source select the aircraft and fund the program. The Air Force needed to be fiscally responsible in their approach of purchasing, maintaining and operating their aircraft in order to gain the "buy-in" of Congress. "Numerous studies show that DOD structure and rapidly changing top management contributed toward weapons that were over cost, behind schedule, and unable to meet mission requirements. The Carnegie Commission on Science, Technology, and Government calculated that overhead alone constitutes 40 percent of the

DOD acquisition budget, compared to 5 to 15 percent in commercial enterprises"

(Battershell, 1999:24). This history cannot be repeated in the C-X program without

economic repercussion. Unfortunately, the Air Force did not meet IOC of the C-X by

1987. However, the Air Force progressed to award the contract to McDonnell Douglas,

and had named the new aircraft the C-17A Globemaster III.

In 1993, the expectations of the C-17A program were not has high as they were

leading up to this point in time. It became apparent that the program was stricken with

financial hardship. By 1993, "estimates of the program's costs had grown by nearly $19

billion, or 47 percent since its inception, excluding the effects of changes in both quantity

and expected inflation" (Congressional Budget Office, 1993:2). Acquisition costs stayed

steady at $40 billion, but the return on investment was significantly cut; no longer will

the $40 billion provide for 210 aircraft, but now 120 aircraft (Congressional Budget

Office, 1993:2). Additionally, the C-17A program was initially forecast for completion

in 1998, but due to setbacks, the revised forecast was for completion of the contract in

2001 (Congressional Budget Office, 1993:2). Delays and costs were out of control and

the Congress noticed this. Thus, the Congressional Budegt Office, was asked to evaluate

and analyze alternatives to the C-17A. In 1993, four alternatives to the C-17A were

conceived in the 1993 Congressional Budget Office Paper, *The C-17A: Costs and

Alternatives.* (Congressional Budget Office, 1993:1):

- Option 1: Buy 60 C-17As at reduced production rates.

- Option 2: Buy 30 C-17As at reduced production rates.

- Option 3: Buy 20 C-17As, restart the C-5B assembly line, and modify the

  wings on the C-141.

- Option 4: Buy 20 C-17As, restart the C-5B assembly line, and purchase new commercial airlift aircraft

In 1993, the C-17A was failing not only in the realm of procurement, but also in its performance capabilities.

The C-17A Program was in dire straits in 1993 moving into 1994. The relationship between the contractor, McDonnell Douglas and the U.S. Government was in gridlock and had "seriously impeded progress" (Kennedy, 2004:130). On 3 January 1994, the Under Secretary of Defense Deutch, wrote John McDonnell of McDonnell Douglas and stated:

> Over the past five months we have performed and intensive review of the C-17A program. Based on this review, I have concluded that the current C-17A program is not viable without substantial change and that three elements of change are required for a successful strategic airlift program: 1. A provisional 2-year program for C-17A production at a rate of 6 aircraft per year. During this period McDonnell Douglas must (a) introduce major mangagement and manufacturing process changes, (b) demonstrate an ability to deliver aircraft on a schedule and at cost, (c) successfully complete the flight test program and (d) satisfy all other contract specifications including Reliability, Maintainability, and Availability (RM & A) requirements. 2. Execution of a comprehensive settlement between the United States Government and McDonnell Douglas on outstanding C-17A business and management issues. This prospective settlement and the management and manufacturing production changes mentioned above are the subject of this letter. 3. Consideration of a mix of commercial wide-body aircraft or new C-5B production to meet the requirements for military airlift in the future….The business settlement in this letter cannot stand alone because by itself it does not accomplish the goal of assuring the nation's strategic airlift military requirement will be met. (Kennedy, 2004:131-132)

Amazingly, McDonnell Douglas, the U.S. Government, and the Air Force were able to bring the C-17A to IOC on 17 January 1995. The actual timeline from AMST to IOC is depcicted in Figure 8.

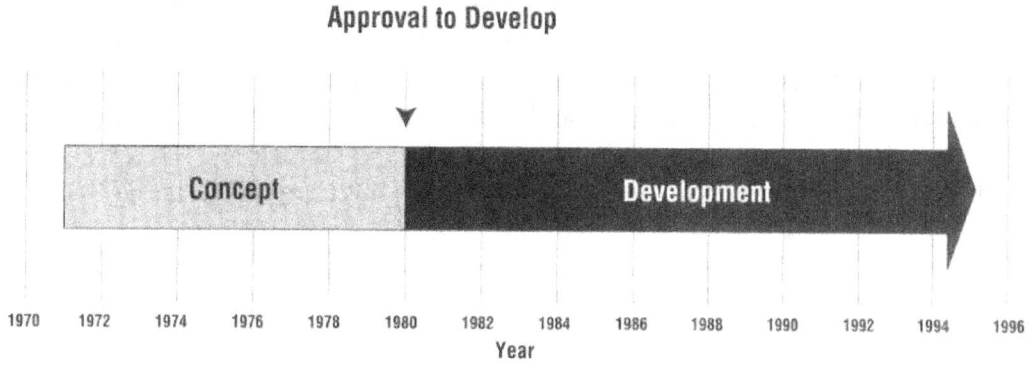

Figure 8: C-17A Concept to Initial Operating Capability (Battershell, 1999:12)

One might say that the rest is history, but the saga continued as Congress and the Air

Force continuously tried to determine the right size of the C-17A fleet. The storied past

of this amazing tactical turned strategic airlift aircraft is not mirrored at all in the process

of developing the Boeing 777, a very capable strategic freighter aircraft. The Boeing

777F is one for consideration by the U.S. Government.

History of the Boeing 777/777F

"In the time it has taken the Air Force to buy the C-17A, Boeing has designed, tested and
produced the 747-400, 757, and 767 and has recently rolled out the new 777."
-Senator Jeff Bingaman (D-NM) (Battershell, 1999:3)

The storied past of the C-17A is not found in the history of the Boeing 777.

Although not without issues the Boeing 777 program was executed on a much smoother

timeline than that of the C-17A. Much like the Air Force, after Boeing decided to

proceed with the 777, they established a program office with the responsibility to

develop, configure, design, validate, and provide definition to the product (Battershell,

1999:41). Boeing defined the 777 as follows:

26

The mission of the 777 is to provide safe and timely worldwide airlift of passengers and cargo in a cost effective manner. It must be comfortable and aesthetically pleasing for passengers. It must operate routinely on a fast-paced schedule with high mechanical reliability and minimum down-time. It must operate efficiently and effectively both in the air and into and out of crowded airfields. And it must have exteneded-range twin-engine operations (ETOPS) capability upon delivery to the customer. (Battershell, 1999:41-42)

The goal for the aircraft was unchanging, the program defnition remained the same during the entire program. During Boeing's market research they "revealed the company needed a plane to fill a gap in the market between the 767-200, which carried 218 passengers, and the 747-400, which carried 419 passengers" (Battershell, 1999:20). The program goal for Boeing was to fill that gap.

The unwavering of the program goals allowed for the Boeing team to continuously work towards a common, unchanging goal. Figure 9 depicts the Boeing aircraft from conception to completion:

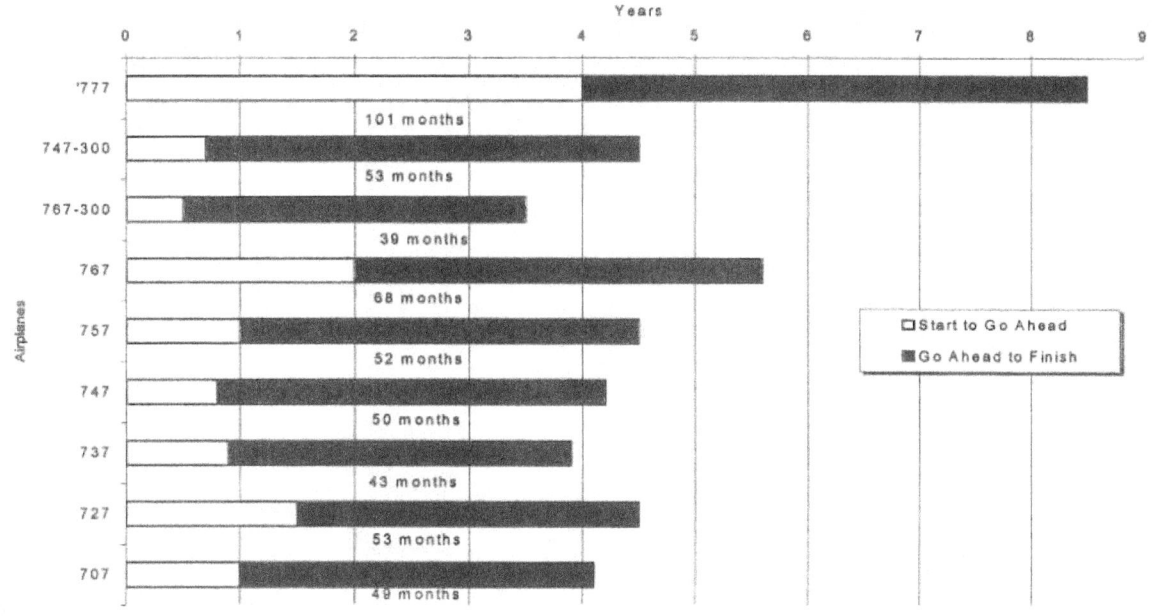

Figure 9: Boeing Aircraft Development Timeline (Battershell, 1999:25)

The Boeing 777 had a defined beginning and a defined end goal, supported by the Boeing team, their mangagement and board of directors, unlike that of the C-17A.

Comparison of the Boeing 777 and the C-17A

The Boeing 777 and the McDonnell Douglas, now Boeing C-17A, both began with a mission. However, the path taken to accomplish their respective mission differed greatly. Both aircraft focused on the mission. For the Boeing 777, the mission was to fill the gap in the passenger aircraft market, for the C-17A, it was to fill the gap in the tactical/strategic airlift requirements. Figure 10 shows how important it is to have a precise idea of the conceptual design of the aircraft. Life cycle cost is the cost of owning, maintaining and operating the aircraft, most of the costs are determined in the beginning of the aircraft development. Comparing Figure 10 with the Figures 11 and 12 show the progress in the design of the two aircraft. The C-17A was developed in 5 stages where

28

the Boeing 777 was developed in 3 stages, and this is after each aircraft was approved either by their respective board or Congress.

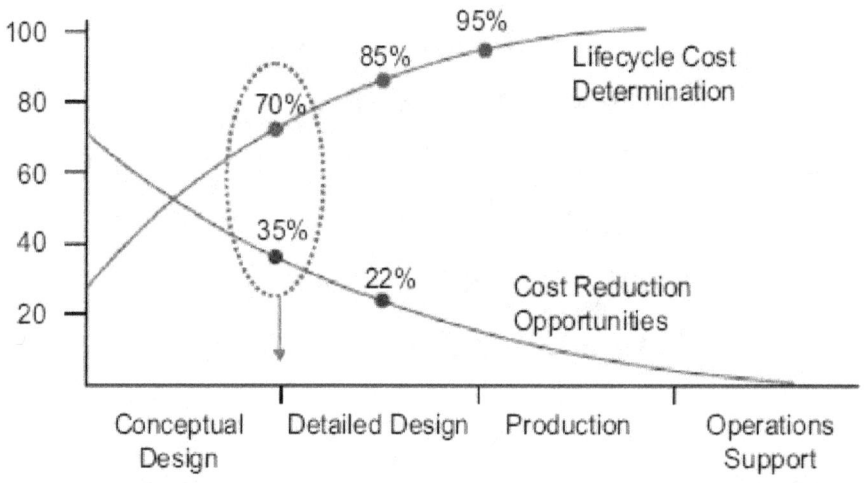

Figure 10: Loss of control over the life cycle (Price, 2006:353)

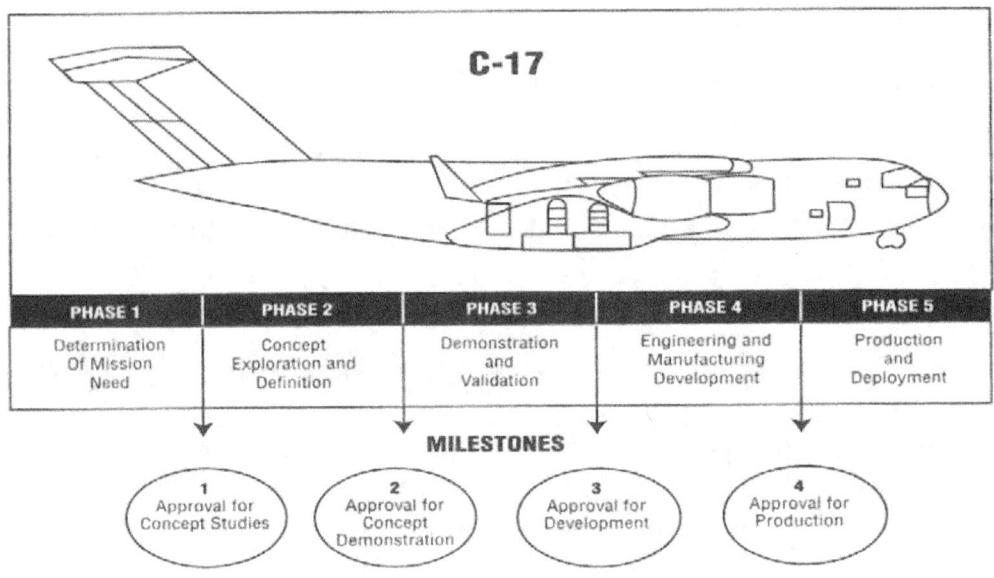

Figure 11: C-17A Development Milestones (Battershell, 1999:59)

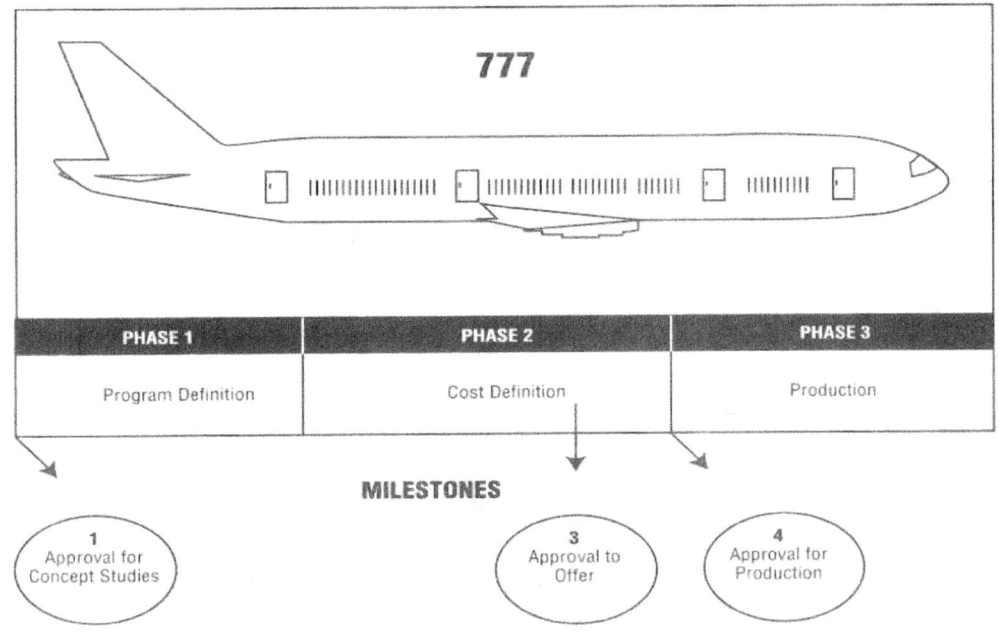

Figure 12: Boeing 777 Development Milestones (Battershell, 1999:58)

Clearly, as displayed in the "loss of life cycle" chart, it is important to have a very clear

idea of what exactly the mission of the aircraft will be prior to getting too far in the

milestones. Boeing had a very clear mission statement from the beginning. The U.S.

Government had a very blurred vision on the intent of the aircraft that morphed over 20

years prior to it being IOC, each iteration incurring more life cycle costs. However, in

the end of both of these processes, two amazing planes have been produced.

Unfortunately, due to the long sustainment period for the conflicts in the Middle East and

Southwest Asia, the C-17A is at risk of being utilized at a rate faster than what was

programmed.

C-17 Overfly

Aircraft are programmed for a certain number of hours to be flown over a

determined time span. According to the Air Force Life Cycle Management Center at

30

Wright Patterson Air Force Base, the C-17 is currently designed for a 30 year/30,000 hour life (Robertson, 2013:email). According to Representative John Runyan, (R-NJ), in questioning General William Fraser, III, USTRANSCOM commander, the C-17 has overflown its program of record by 21 percent (HASC testimony, 6 March 2013: http://armedservices.granicus.com/ViewPublisher.php?view_id=2). Although not at the same level of overflight, Figure 13 shows an overflight of approximately 5%.

Year	Programmed Flight Hours	Actual Flight Hours
1998	46365	42623
1999	57505	56677
2000	82816	58423
2001	86883	81071
2002	105090	109877
2003	127121	159835
2004	146493	155752
2005	158598	157753
2006	170129	158855
2007	181798	177297
2008	193698	187249
2009	198261	213986
2010	185357	231269
2011	187455	220996
2012	175426	202124
Total	2102995	2213787
	C-17 Overfly	105.27%

Figure 13: C-17 Programmed vs Actual Flight Hours, 1998-2012 (AMC/AA9, March 2013)

Although the overfly discrepancy between what is referenced by Representative Runyan and the flight hours referenced in Figure 13, is quite large, the reality is that the C-17A is in a current overfly status. Regardless of the actual percentage of overfly, the Air Force Life Cycle Mangagemet Center is already considering options to increase the life cycle of the C-17A to 60,000 hours (Robertson, 2013:email). The Service Life Extension Program (SLEP) for aircraft is usually very expensive, as is the cost of fuel. The Air Force needs to focus on minimizing SLEPs for aircraft and maximizing fuel efficiency, even if that includes purchasing more aircraft to optimize the strategic airlift fleet.

Energy Future

A running joke among pilots and Petroleum, Oils and Lubricants airmen goes like this: "What is an aircraft without fuel?"; the answer is a "static display". Static displays don't serve the Air Force or the United States very well during times of conflict or an all out war. A quick discussion about this around the dinner table might include three results of wasteful fuel usage: 1. We run out of available fuel; 2. We use so much fuel we drive the price of fuel to the point where it is not affordable; or, 3. We run out of our programmed fuel expenditures. According to Dr. Mark T. Maybury, chief scientist of the United States Air Force, "the Air Force faces daunting energy challenges that promise only to increase in severity, given the increased global demand for energy, diminishing global energy supplies, and demands for enhanced environmental stewardship" (Maybury, 2012:3). With recent conflicts in North Africa and the "Arab Spring", this severity, as mentioned by Dr. Maybury, may be understated: we are not facing "daunting" energy challenges, but are facing life changing energy challenges. The Air Force corporation must efficiently use its resources, both the aircraft and the fuel.

Efficient use of resources is not a new idea, but sometimes slow to percolate through all aspects of operating. Often the "cost of doing business" is the easy answer and often not the most efficient way of operating. In the world of delivering goods to the

32

troop in need, often effectiveness is the only concern. As show in Figure 14, the primary expense for energy in the Air Force is Aviation fuel.

In a company situation, the president would first consider saving money by attacking the biggest drain on their budget. You cannot make many changes in fixed costs, but variable costs allow for potential savings. One of the largest variable costs in the Air Force is fuel. Understandably, though, the Air Force would prefer to have airplanes accomplishing their mission instead of being on a continous state of static display. Maybury (2010) suggests that the C-17A and the F-35 are the biggest current and projected users of Air Force fuel (Figure 15). In sequence with this knowledge, that is where research should be focused to look for alternatives and efficiencies, namely in the palletized cargo transport.

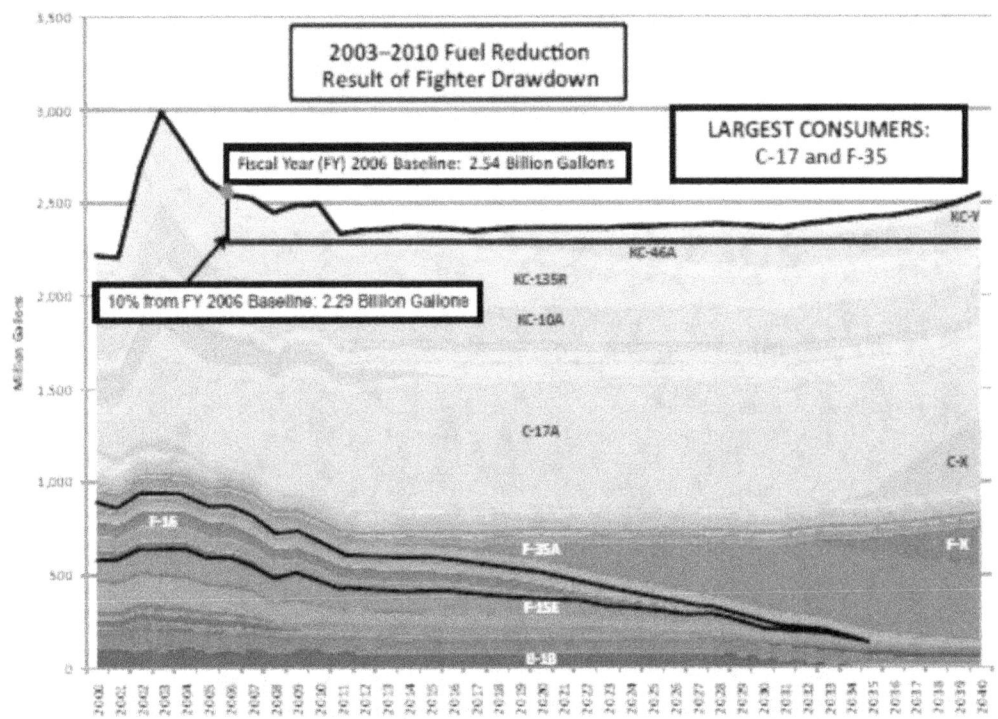

Figure 15: Air Force Fuel Burn Projections (Maybury, 2010: 5)

With the knowledge of where our biggest energy drains occur, it is simple to determine where our biggest gains might occur. Outside of proclaiming that Air Force flight operations halt, there are progressive ideas in circulation to minimize fuel costs in aircraft operation that do not include purchasing more efficient aircraft.

Changing behavior, must be preceded by preparing the culture to change. The Air Force is preparing for change with Air Energy initiatives (Figure 16). The charge of finding savings in the utilization of energy, not only falls on the military, but also the aviation industry. The Air Force has chosen to lead the development in certain areas like center of gravity control (Maybury, 2010:6). Other areas, the Air Force has chosen to follow industry. One such area that the Air Force has chosen to follow is that of lifting bodies (Maybury, 2010:6). Figure 16 below shows some of the current initiatives.

34

Efficiency in aviation is the responsibility of all involved from industry, to military, to commercial aviation, including the airlines. Unfortunately, as aircraft are built with added capabilities the corresoponding fuel burn usually also increases.

Fuel price increases usually lead to seeking more fuel efficient vehicles. In the case of the Air Force, this is not true. "Operational improvements to new platforms such as the C-17A and the F-35 come with burn rates 50 percent to 125 percent more than those of legacy platforms such as the C-141 and F-16" (Maybury, 2010:4). Current and historical fuel prices are displayed in Figure 17 below, showing an upward trend in fuel prices. The chart that follows in Figure 18 also shows an upward trend in fuel costs.

The Air Force will not get rid of the C-17A or the F-35, due to fuel costs alone, but to utilize the aircraft in a different manner is an appropriate expectation.

The focus of this research is on transport aircraft and the large amount of fuel the aircraft burns. According to Erin C. Conaton, in a 2010 speech on "A New Culture: Energy as an Operations Enabler", the Undersecretary of the Air Force stated that Air Mobility Command, and specifically Mobility Air Forces (cargo and air refueling aircraft), "account for more that 50% of the fuel used by the Air Force" and the Air Force in 2010 dollars would spend about 6.7 billion in aviation fuel (Conaton, 2010:speech). Efficiencies in tranportation of our palletized cargo must be utilized.

Mobility Efficiency

Efficiency is a goal of every corporation, business or military, regardless of type or country of origin. There is no such case where producing a continuous effect regardless of cost is an option—eventually the bills will have to be paid or the credit card will be at its maximum limit. In essence, being efficient is preserving an effect for future use. If you are not efficient, then how can you ensure a future effect? According to the Merriam-Webster Online Dictionary, efficient is defined as "1. Being or involving the immediate agent in producing an effect; 2. Productive of desired effects; especially productive without waste; an *efficient* worker" (Merriam-Webster, 2013:website). This efficiency was not necessarily in the fore-front of those executing the Berlin Airlift or perhaps even more recent Operation ENDURING FREEDOM or Operation IRAQI FREEDOM.

Initial times of war or conflict are not time to seek effiecient mobility operations, supplies and troops must be exactly where requested, regardless of cost. However, times of sustainment during war, must be treated differently. If those times of sustainment are not treated differently, then how does a military prepare or save resources required to disregard efficiency and seek only effect when the next crisis arises?

The definition of efficient actually includes the word effect. To be efficient you actually cause an effect. But to be effective, does not include being efficient. Consider when you drive a car. One can be effective and drive from Point A to Point B and deliver the required goods, regardless if the trunk is full or not, as fast as possible. In this case one is only causing an effect: delivery of goods as quick as possible. Effectiveness is not directly linked to efficiency.

Effectiveness does not lead to efficiency; nor does efficiency necessarily lead to effectiveness. But, proactive decision making can increase efficiency at minimal or no impact to effectiveness. The money saved from a consolidated shipment and perhaps excess wear and tear on the vehicle actually is preserving a future effect while being efficienct and causing a current effect. Sustainment operations, especially in times of extended conflict, are clearly an opportunity to seek effiecient operations—as a military and government there is no other option.

Other Research Comparing Aircraft on Fuel Burn

After a thorough literature review, no research was found evaulating aircraft on their performance and operating costs that does not require proprietary information to do a comparison of the C-17A and the Boeing 777F. This may be due to the limited research assets available or because a lot of that information may be proprietary. Therefore, the research is completed using a comparative cost analysis based purely on fuel burn on equal or exact routes.

Summary

The history of airlift, the amazing start with the Berlin Airlift and resulting in the airlift capabilities of today, to bring huge tanks to austere locations and to carry an incredible amount of pallets in an effective manner is simply amazing. However, it is time to re-evaluate airlift operations and seek an enduring efficiency in order to protect the required capabilities of airlift.

III. Methodology

"Our failure to get broad agreement as to what the mobility requirement is and how best to satisfy it has caused the traditional advocacy process for airlift modernization to be ineffective." Stated by the Air Force in its *Airlift Modernization: A Different Approach;* (Kennedy, 2004: 23)

Chapter Overview

This chapter discusses Comparative Cost Analysis the methodology that was used in accomplishing the research.

Test Subjects

Two aircraft, the Boeing C-17A and Boeing 777F, are evaluated in this study. The evaluation is on fuel burn only due to the limited amount of data. Fuel burn is utilized, because fuel usage is currently a "hot-ticket" item in the United States and in the government.

Assumptions

There are several assumptions in this research.

1. All of the C-17A data provided from the Fuel Efficiency Office at Air Mobility Command is correct.

2. The C-17A and the 777F are operated as per specified Technical Order and operated in the most efficient manner possible.

3. The Air Force will not change how they manage their cargo at the ports and the aircraft will maintain the same load factors as done historically.

4. The cargo loading system on the Boeing 777F will be able to support the 463L pallet that is used on the C-17A.

5. In order to increase the amount of data available for the comparison of the 777F and the C-17A on a specific route, Ramstein Air Base and Spangdahlem Air Base are equal distant from Dover AFB.

6. Gross payload is the payload for the aircraft, not the revenue payload.

7. All the cargo carried on the C-17A was palletized cargo.

Process

The flight data for the C-17A was retrieved from the Mobility Air Force (MAF) Fuel Tracker database on 10 December 2012. The data encompasses 1 January 2009 until 14 November 2012. The data was filtered to include only missions to ETAR (Ramstein Air Base, Germany) and ETAD (Spangdahlem Air Base, Germany). ETAR and ETAD are utilized due to the fact that thousands of C-17A's transit these airfields every year due to the continuous sustainment operations in the Middle East and Southwest Asia, namely in Iraq and Afghanistan. The data was then filtered further to delete all diverted missions into ETAR or ETAD.

Next, all missions that accomplished air refueling are deleted. These data points are deleted in order to ensure a reliable fuel burn is utilized in the analysis. Then the data was filtered to only have departures that started with a "K" indicating that the mission originated from a United States ICAO airfield. After doing this filter and deletion of unneeded data points (those that diverted to ETAR/ETAD and those that refueled), 4,030 data points (flights) remained.

Each data point contains mission identification, mission class, mission design series, tail number of aircraft, departure airport ICAO, arrival airport ICAO, actual departure time (in Zulu), actual arrival time (in Zulu), actual flight time, actual ramp fuel (in thousands of pounds), actual landing fuel (in thousands of pounds), actual fuel used (in thousands of pounds) and actual cargo weight (in thousands of pounds).

After filtering the data to the 4,030 remaining flights, the researcher evaluated the data to find the most common routes between the East coast and ETAR/ETAD. It was found that the most common route between ETAR/ETAD is with an origination from Dover Air Force Base, Delaware (KDOV). It makes sense that most of the flights originated from KDOV, because it is a primary port for cargo movement in the United States. Between KDOV and ETAR/ETAD, there are 1,219 flights: 571 flights are between KDOV and ETAD; and, 648 flights between KDOV and ETAR.

The next step in the analysis was to average the duration between KDOV and ETAR, KDOV and ETAD, and KDOV and ETAR/ETAD. The cargo weight was then averaged to include both KDOV to ETAR and ETAD. This average weight is referred to as the "normal" C-17A cargo weight thus further. The "normal" C-17A cargo weight was compared to that of the average of all 4,030 lines of data and was found that the "normal" weight is 4.8K pounds more than the average of all flights from the United States to ETAR/ETAD. Since the "normal" C-17A cargo weight is more conservative, it was chosen to be used for analysis.

After determining the duration of the baseline flight and the "normal" cargo weight of the C-17A, the maximum, unrefueled capability of the C-17A between KDOV and ETAR was identified. The AMC Fuel Efficiency Office provided a flight plan between KDOV and ETAR at that maximum cargo capability without air refueling during that flight. The flight plan was "run" on 4 December 2012, using current atmospheric conditions at that point in time. One potential downfall to using this data is that winter-time jet streams are normally very strong and provide a strong tailwind between KDOV and ETAR. However, it is acceptable in this case, because it provides "best-case" and thus the most conservative C-17A max weight data.

Real world fuel burn from the data is used instead of using the planning factors in the AFPAM10-1403. The fuel burn rates of the AFPAM10-1403 are stated in Figure 19.

Aircraft Type	Fuel Burn Rate (lbs/hr)	Aircraft Type	Fuel Burn Rate (lbs/hr)	Aircraft Type	Fuel Burn Rate (lbs/hr)
C-130	4,533	B-747	26,800	F-15E	13,244
C-130J	4,500	B-767	10,552	F-16	5,795
C-17	21,097	B-777	14,305	A/OA-10	3,996
C-5	24,033	DC-8	13,916	F/A-18C/D	7,417
C-5M	22,110	DC-10	20,616	F/A-18E/F	8,623
KC-10	18,948	MD-11	17,511	EA-6B	7,102
KC-135R	11,291	F-22A	11,118	E-6A/B	10,747
A-330	10,260	F-15C	11,189	AV-8B	5,461

NOTE: Fuel burn rates extracted from AFPAM 23-221, Fuels Logistics Planning, 22 December 2006 (converted to lbs/hr using 6.7 lbs/gal conversion rate). Fuel burn rates are for planning purposes only. Actual rate varies according to mission profile, AC model, configuration, altitude, airspeed etc.

Figure 19: Fuel Burn Rates According to AFPAM 10-1403 (AFPAM 10-1403, 2011:17)

From experience, the 10-1403 fuel burn rates are not very reliable. The researcher used to fly the KC-135R as an instructor pilot at the schoolhouse, and one would usually only see fuel burns of 11,291 pounds per hour when you did pattern work like radar approaches and touch and go's; a normal mission would be planned at 10,000 pounds of fuel burned an hour. Also, according to a former schoolhouse instructor for the C-17A, when he flew an 8 hour mission he would plan to burn 20,000 pounds of fuel an hour when it included pattern work, so a mission with extended cruise time would be less (Wick, 2012). Additionally, the fuel burn of aircraft changes significantly based on how much cargo an aircraft is carrying. A lighter aircraft burns less than a heavier aircraft. It is not apparent in these tables, or in the referenced AFPAM 23-221, what the gross weight of the aircraft was for the fuel burn calculations in the 10-1403. For these reasons, the AFPAM Fuel Burn Rates are not used in the analysis section.

Total flight time is calculated by using a decimal system that is utilized and accepted in all aviation related activities. For the Air Force, this process is found in the *AEROSPACE EQUIPMENT MAINTENANCE INSPECTION, DOCUMENTATION, POLICIES, AND PROCEDURES,* TO-00-20-1. The document for calculating flight time is shown in Figure 20.

CONVERSION		
Minutes		Dur
1 ~ 2	=	0
3 ~ 8	=	.1
9 ~ 14	=	2
15 ~ 20	=	3
21 ~ 26	=	4
27 ~ 33	=	5
34 ~ 39	=	6
40 ~ 45	=	7
46 ~ 51	=	8
52 ~ 57	=	9
58 ~ 60	=	Next

Figure 20: Flight Hours Conversion Table (TO-00-20-1, 15 June 2011:5-3)

Flight hours are calculated by whole hours plus the additional minutes. As an example, a 1 hour and 34 minute flight would be considered a 1.6 total duration. Flight times are referenced in this manner in the analysis. Next, it was necessary to obtain critical Boeing 777F flight performance data.

Boeing 777F data was provided by the Aircraft Engineer and Tech Planning division of a multinational air freight company that operates the Boeing 777F. Most operating data, except sales data, from Boeing is considered proprietary and not possible to retrieve for this research. The multinational air freight company that operates the Boeing 777F has graciously provided fuel and flight data utilizing their current Boeing 777F flight data, which includes historical winds, flight altitudes and flight airspeeds. This data combined enabled access to very accurate, non-proprietary, flight data.

The multinational air freight company provided the researcher with flight data with the aircraft loaded at the maximum weight capable for a flight between KDOV and ETAR. Additionally, they provided flight data at the reduced "normal" C-17A weight. After the baseline flights for both the C-17A and the 777F were established at "normal" and maximum weights, the next step is to evaluate the fuel burn of each aircraft.

Fuel burn for a C-17A loaded at the "normal" rate on the KDOV to ETAR/ETAD flight profile was obtained by taking the total fuel burned per flight and dividing it by the flight duration to determine a fuel burn in pounds of fuel per hour (lbs/hr) for each flight. After the fuel burn per hour was determined, the average fuel burned per flight was determined. The fuel burned per flight was determined by utilizing the total fuel burned per flight for all 1,219 flights and averaging those fuel utilization numbers. Fuel burn for the maximum weight C-17A flight was determined from the flight plan provided by the AMC Fuel Efficiency Office. To obtain the fuel burned per hour for the maximum weight C-17A, the total fuel used was divided by the total flight duration.

The fuel burn data for the Boeing 777F was obtained from the excel worksheet provided by the multinational air freight company. On the worksheet, they provided total fuel burned in pounds and fuel burn per hour in pounds. These calculations were provided for both the maximum weight 777F and for the "normal" cargo weight.

After fuel burn per hour and per flight was established, it was then time to determine the fuel utilized per pound of cargo. The fuel burned for the "normal" weight and the maximum cargo weight for each of the aircraft was divided by their respective cargo weights. This calculation resulted in a ratio of pounds of fuel burned for each pound of cargo moved from KDOV to ETAR/ETAD. The next step in the analysis was to determine the cost of moving each pound of cargo from KDOV to ETAR/ETAD based on the two different aircraft at the two different load factors. The cost is based on fuel costs alone.

The fuel cost per gallon is used. The price that is used is the Defense Logistics Agency (DLA) standard price. The current and historical prices were obtained from DLA – Finance Energy on 5 March 2013. The current price Fiscal Year 2013 price per gallon of JP-8 as of 1 Oct 2012 is $3.73 per gallon. The cost of JP-8 per gallon was then divided by 6.7 pounds, which is the weight of a gallon of JP-8. This was done to determine the cost of one pound of fuel. Afterwards, this cost per pound of fuel was used to determine the cost of moving one pound of cargo depending on the aircraft and cargo load. This was done by multiplying the ratio of fuel used per pound of cargo by the cost of a pound of fuel.

After the determination was made of how much it cost to move a pound of cargo, the next step was to determine how much the fuel cost for the entire mission to move the maximum load or the "normal" load on each respective aircraft. This was accomplished by utilizing the total fuel burn produced either by the average of the total fuel burn data for the "normal" cargo load for the C-17A, the C-17A maximum weight flight plan and from the total gallons burned by the Boeing 777F.

The next and final step was to determine how many flights it would take to pay off a Boeing 777F in just the fuel savings of the aircraft alone. In this determination, the calculation was done using the most conservative method possible; it was accomplished by using the "normal" payload fuel savings. It is impossible to take into account the extra capacity capability in the Boeing 777F and do a true fuel burn comparison as the maximum cargo weight of the aircraft are different. Thus, comparing the C-17A versus the Boeing 777F at the "normal" weight is the only way to accomplish a true comparison. The cost in fuel for the "normal" weight Boeing 777F is subtracted from the cost in fuel from the "normal" weight C-17A. The next step was to determine the number of available flights each year.

In order to create a "payoff" time, it was first necessary to access how many flight hours are available each year and overall to the C-17A program. Next, the hours were turned into flights, by using the average time of the flight being 7.9 hrs. The payoff was then converted into the number of flights between KDOV and ETAR/ETAD.

An additional "payoff" was also calculated to take advantage of the fact the Boeing 777F flies faster than the C-17A. A 7.9 flight for the C-17A, takes 7.02 hours for the Boeing 777F. This reduced flight time was then converted into monetary savings by multiplying .88 flight hours by the cost per flight hour. This additional savings was then added to the difference in cost per flight hour. This was then utilized to create another "payoff" time for a Boeing 777F aircraft.

Summary

The methodology is overall very simple; however, it all depends of the ability to gain information that can be difficult to obtain. The Boeing website offers a lot of data online; however, it does not discuss the real world operating performance of their aircraft. Thus, it was critical to obtain real world Boeing 777F operating data. The methodology is simple and is credible in accomplishing a cost comparison of the two aircraft based on one factor, fuel burn.

IV. Analysis and Results

Chapter Overview

The analysis of this data is done in a couple different ways. The analysis focused on the fuel burn and cost of each aircraft at their specific weights, the first being a "normal weight" and the second being a max cargo weight. The route chosen for the analysis was that between KDOV and ETAR or ETAD.

Capabilities Comparison

Before delving further into the analysis, the capabilities of the two aircraft is important to establish (Figure 21).

Results of Scenarios

The aircraft are analyzed using two different cargo loads. The first load was the "normal" payload of the C-17A between KDOV and ETAR/ETAD, which is 56.4K pounds. The other weight evaluated is the maximum weight, which is the maximum cargo weight the aircraft, either the C-17A or the Boeing 777F, can carry from KDOV to ETAR/ETAD without refueling or exceeding the maximum weight of the aircraft. The maximum weights are in Figure 21. Regardless of the weight evaluated, the Boeing 777F is the better option for oceanic palletized cargo movement.

Clearly the Boeing 777F utilized up to is maximum cargo capability on the KDOV to ETAR route is the most efficient option when shipping an article through the air cargo system. Not only is the aircraft more capable in moving pallets across the ocean (Figure 21), but the 777F is also more efficient as evident in the cost to move 1 pound of cargo (Figure 22).

Investigative Questions Answered

1.   At what fuel price point would it make sense to actually purchase and operate the new oceanic airlift aircraft?

Fuel is a very expensive part of aviation. Fuel prices have risen so much that fuel is now a consideration in purchasing everything from a generator to a car. In the case of comparing the C-17A and the Boeing 777F, fuel savings can be found at any price point for fuel. Analysis was completed with JP-8 costing $2.80 a gallon up to a price point of $5.00 a gallon, in 5 cent increments. Additionally, a price point was considered at the current day cost of fuel of $3.73 (DLA Finance, 2013:email). Table 1 below shows the cost in fuel, per flight between KDOV and ETAR/ETAD for a C-17A at its "normal" cargo weight of 56.4K pounds and its maximum weight of 140.5K pounds. Table 2 shows the cost in fuel, per flight between KDOV and ETAR for a Boeing 777F at its "normal" cargo weight of 56.4K pounds and its maximum cargo weight of 233.3K pounds. Table 3 shows the cost comparison of the C-17A and the Boeing 777F carrying the "normal" payload.

Normally as weights of aircraft increase more fuel is burned. In the case of the C-17A, note that the data does not show an increase of fuel burn when comparing the cost of the "normal" weight and the maximum weight. This is a difference in the "real world" data acquired from actual flights and the current flight planning software. Higher weight payload does not burn less fuel—it simply is impossible, it takes fuel to move stuff; the more stuff the more fuel. There is currently unpublished research that discusses C-17 flight planning software may not be accurate. The Boeing 777F data demonstrates that more fuel is burned as the aircraft gets heavier, as demonstrated by the increased costs.

Table 1: Single Flight Costs (KDOV-ETAR) C-17A "Reduced" Weight and Maximum Weight

Cost of Fuel	C-17A "Normal Weight"	C-17 Maximum Weight
$2.80	$59,644.50	$56,443.82
$2.85	$60,709.58	$57,451.75
$2.90	$61,774.66	$58,459.67
$2.95	$62,839.74	$59,467.60
$3.00	$63,904.82	$60,475.52
$3.05	$64,969.90	$61,483.45
$3.10	$66,034.98	$62,491.37
$3.15	$67,100.06	$63,499.30
$3.20	$68,165.14	$64,507.22
$3.25	$69,230.22	$65,515.15
$3.30	$70,295.30	$66,523.07
$3.35	$71,360.38	$67,531.00
$3.40	$72,425.46	$68,538.93
$3.45	$73,490.54	$69,546.85
$3.50	$74,555.62	$70,554.78
$3.55	$75,620.70	$71,562.70
$3.60	$76,685.78	$72,570.63
$3.65	$77,750.86	$73,578.55
$3.70	$78,815.95	$74,586.48
$3.73	$79,454.99	$75,191.23
$3.75	$79,881.03	$75,594.40
$3.80	$80,946.11	$76,602.33
$3.85	$82,011.19	$77,610.25
$3.90	$83,076.27	$78,618.18
$3.95	$84,141.35	$79,626.10
$4.00	$85,206.43	$80,634.03
$4.05	$86,271.51	$81,641.96
$4.10	$87,336.59	$82,649.88
$4.15	$88,401.67	$83,657.81
$4.20	$89,466.75	$84,665.73
$4.25	$90,531.83	$85,673.66
$4.30	$91,596.91	$86,681.58
$4.35	$92,661.99	$87,689.51
$4.40	$93,727.07	$88,697.43
$4.45	$94,792.15	$89,705.36
$4.50	$95,857.23	$90,713.28
$4.55	$96,922.31	$91,721.21
$4.60	$97,987.39	$92,729.13
$4.65	$99,052.47	$93,737.06
$4.70	$100,117.55	$94,744.99
$4.75	$101,182.63	$95,752.91
$4.80	$102,247.71	$96,760.84
$4.85	$103,312.79	$97,768.76
$4.90	$104,377.87	$98,776.69
$4.95	$105,442.95	$99,784.61
$5.00	$106,508.03	$100,792.54

54

Table 2: Single Flight Costs (KDOV-ETAR) Boeing 777F "Reduced" Weight and Maximum Weight

Cost of Fuel	Boeing 777F "Normal" Weight	Boeing 777F Maximum Weight
$2.80	$37,493.67	$52,661.31
$2.85	$38,163.20	$53,601.69
$2.90	$38,832.73	$54,542.07
$2.95	$39,502.26	$55,482.46
$3.00	$40,171.79	$56,422.84
$3.05	$40,841.32	$57,363.22
$3.10	$41,510.85	$58,303.60
$3.15	$42,180.38	$59,243.98
$3.20	$42,849.91	$60,184.36
$3.25	$43,519.44	$61,124.74
$3.30	$44,188.97	$62,065.12
$3.35	$44,858.50	$63,005.50
$3.40	$45,528.03	$63,945.88
$3.45	$46,197.56	$64,886.26
$3.50	$46,867.09	$65,826.64
$3.55	$47,536.62	$66,767.02
$3.60	$48,206.15	$67,707.40
$3.65	$48,875.68	$68,647.78
$3.70	$49,545.21	$69,588.16
$3.73	$49,946.93	$70,152.39
$3.75	$50,214.74	$70,528.54
$3.80	$50,884.27	$71,468.93
$3.85	$51,553.80	$72,409.31
$3.90	$52,223.33	$73,349.69
$3.95	$52,892.86	$74,290.07
$4.00	$53,562.39	$75,230.45
$4.05	$54,231.92	$76,170.83
$4.10	$54,901.45	$77,111.21
$4.15	$55,570.98	$78,051.59
$4.20	$56,240.51	$78,991.97
$4.25	$56,910.04	$79,932.35
$4.30	$57,579.57	$80,872.73
$4.35	$58,249.10	$81,813.11
$4.40	$58,918.63	$82,753.49
$4.45	$59,588.16	$83,693.87
$4.50	$60,257.69	$84,634.25
$4.55	$60,927.22	$85,574.63
$4.60	$61,596.75	$86,515.01
$4.65	$62,266.28	$87,455.40
$4.70	$62,935.81	$88,395.78
$4.75	$63,605.34	$89,336.16
$4.80	$64,274.87	$90,276.54
$4.85	$64,944.40	$91,216.92
$4.90	$65,613.93	$92,157.30
$4.95	$66,283.46	$93,097.68
$5.00	$66,952.99	$94,038.06

Table 3: Single Flight Fuel Costs (KDOV-ETAR) C-17A versus Boeing 777F "Normal" Weight

Cost of Fuel	C-17A "Normal" Weight	Boeing 777F "Normal" Weight
$2.80	$59,644.50	$37,493.67
$2.85	$60,709.58	$38,163.20
$2.90	$61,774.66	$38,832.73
$2.95	$62,839.74	$39,502.26
$3.00	$63,904.82	$40,171.79
$3.05	$64,969.90	$40,841.32
$3.10	$66,034.98	$41,510.85
$3.15	$67,100.06	$42,180.38
$3.20	$68,165.14	$42,849.91
$3.25	$69,230.22	$43,519.44
$3.30	$70,295.30	$44,188.97
$3.35	$71,360.38	$44,858.50
$3.40	$72,425.46	$45,528.03
$3.45	$73,490.54	$46,197.56
$3.50	$74,555.62	$46,867.09
$3.55	$75,620.70	$47,536.62
$3.60	$76,685.78	$48,206.15
$3.65	$77,750.86	$48,875.68
$3.70	$78,815.95	$49,545.21
$3.73	$79,454.99	$49,946.93
$3.75	$79,881.03	$50,214.74
$3.80	$80,946.11	$50,884.27
$3.85	$82,011.19	$51,553.80
$3.90	$83,076.27	$52,223.33
$3.95	$84,141.35	$52,892.86
$4.00	$85,206.43	$53,562.39
$4.05	$86,271.51	$54,231.92
$4.10	$87,336.59	$54,901.45
$4.15	$88,401.67	$55,570.98
$4.20	$89,466.75	$56,240.51
$4.25	$90,531.83	$56,910.04
$4.30	$91,596.91	$57,579.57
$4.35	$92,661.99	$58,249.10
$4.40	$93,727.07	$58,918.63
$4.45	$94,792.15	$59,588.16
$4.50	$95,857.23	$60,257.69
$4.55	$96,922.31	$60,927.22
$4.60	$97,987.39	$61,596.75
$4.65	$99,052.47	$62,266.28
$4.70	$100,117.55	$62,935.81
$4.75	$101,182.63	$63,605.34
$4.80	$102,247.71	$64,274.87
$4.85	$103,312.79	$64,944.40
$4.90	$104,377.87	$65,613.93
$4.95	$105,442.95	$66,283.46
$5.00	$106,508.03	$66,952.99

2.   Which aircraft is more efficient in carrying palletized cargo?

As stated previously in the Literature Review, one of the definitions of efficiency is being "productive of desired effects; especially productive without waste" (Merriam-Webster, 2013:website). In comparing the two aircraft, waste is defined as burning excess fuel per pound of cargo moved from KDOV to ETAR. Figure 22 shows the cost to move one pound of cargo between KDOV and ETAR, for various costs in fuel per gallon.

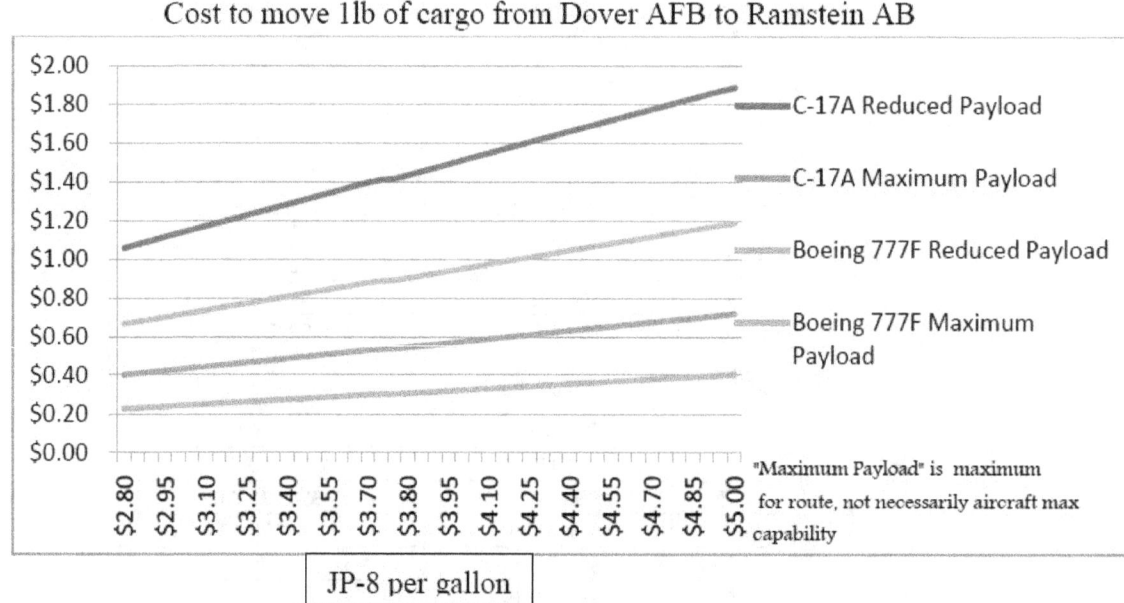

Figure 22: Cost to move 1 pound of cargo

The following table, Table 5, shows the costs to move one pound of cargo for the four different scenarios.

Table 4: Cost to Move 1 pound of cargo from KDOV to ETAR

Cost of Fuel	C-17 "Reduced" Weight	B777F "Reduced Weight	C-17 Max Weight	B777F Max Weight
$2.80	$1.06	$0.66	$0.40	$0.23
$2.85	$1.08	$0.68	$0.41	$0.23
$2.90	$1.10	$0.69	$0.42	$0.23
$2.95	$1.11	$0.70	$0.42	$0.24
$3.00	$1.13	$0.71	$0.43	$0.24
$3.05	$1.15	$0.72	$0.44	$0.25
$3.10	$1.17	$0.74	$0.44	$0.25
$3.15	$1.19	$0.75	$0.45	$0.25
$3.20	$1.21	$0.76	$0.46	$0.26
$3.25	$1.23	$0.77	$0.47	$0.26
$3.30	$1.25	$0.78	$0.47	$0.27
$3.35	$1.27	$0.80	$0.48	$0.27
$3.40	$1.28	$0.81	$0.49	$0.27
$3.45	$1.30	$0.82	$0.49	$0.28
$3.50	$1.32	$0.83	$0.50	$0.28
$3.55	$1.34	$0.84	$0.51	$0.29
$3.60	$1.36	$0.85	$0.52	$0.29
$3.65	$1.38	$0.87	$0.52	$0.29
$3.70	$1.40	$0.88	$0.53	$0.30
$3.73	$1.41	$0.89	$0.54	$0.30
$3.75	$1.42	$0.89	$0.54	$0.30
$3.80	$1.44	$0.90	$0.55	$0.31
$3.85	$1.45	$0.91	$0.55	$0.31
$3.90	$1.47	$0.93	$0.56	$0.31
$3.95	$1.49	$0.94	$0.57	$0.32
$4.00	$1.51	$0.95	$0.57	$0.32
$4.05	$1.53	$0.96	$0.58	$0.33
$4.10	$1.55	$0.97	$0.59	$0.33
$4.15	$1.57	$0.99	$0.60	$0.33
$4.20	$1.59	$1.00	$0.60	$0.34
$4.25	$1.61	$1.01	$0.61	$0.34
$4.30	$1.62	$1.02	$0.62	$0.35
$4.35	$1.64	$1.03	$0.62	$0.35
$4.40	$1.66	$1.04	$0.63	$0.35
$4.45	$1.68	$1.06	$0.64	$0.36
$4.50	$1.70	$1.07	$0.65	$0.36
$4.55	$1.72	$1.08	$0.65	$0.37
$4.60	$1.74	$1.09	$0.66	$0.37
$4.65	$1.76	$1.10	$0.67	$0.37
$4.70	$1.78	$1.12	$0.67	$0.38
$4.75	$1.79	$1.13	$0.68	$0.38
$4.80	$1.81	$1.14	$0.69	$0.39
$4.85	$1.83	$1.15	$0.70	$0.39
$4.90	$1.85	$1.16	$0.70	$0.40
$4.95	$1.87	$1.18	$0.71	$0.40
$5.00	$1.89	$1.19	$0.72	$0.40

3.   Which aircraft is more effective in carrying palletized cargo?

Effectiveness is a word that, when used, implies that a desired outcome was expected or wanted of a certain action. According to Webster's Dictionary, effective means "producing a decided, decisive, or desired effect" (Merriam-Webster, 2013:website). In this study, effectiveness for the C-17A and the Boeing 777F is quantified as the capability to move pallets. The more pallets the aircraft can carry across the ocean, the more effective the aircraft. Referencing Figure 21, the Boeing 777F is more effective in carrying pallets. The C-17A is capable of carrying 18 full-size pallets. The Boeing 777F is able to carry 27 contoured pallets and 10 belly pallets up to 64 inches tall. For an equal comparison, consider the 10 belly pallets to be 5 full pallets; in that case, the Boeing 777F carries 32 full pallets versus the C-17 which carries 18. The Boeing 777F is more effective aircraft for moving pallets than the C-17.

4.   Will the inclusion of this new oceanic airlift aircraft reduce or minimize the need for costly C-17 overhauls or extended depots?

The inclusion of the Boeing 777F, will delay, limit or even eliminate the need for some C-17 overhauls depending on the planned extension of the C-17 life cycle. The life cycle is based upon hours flown or age of aircraft; since the C-17A has been flown at an excessive rate, it is reasonable to believe that they are accelerating towards their 30,000 hour life cycle. If the C-17A is not flying due to the Boeing 777F being utilized to palletized movement, then the progression towards the 30,000 flight hour limit is slowed. Unfortunately, the data is currently not available to make final determinations with regards to the extent of a delay, limitation or elimination, as it seems the discussion is still in the infancy stages. It cannot be denied however that the inclusion of an oceanic or long haul freighter designated for pallets would contribute to delaying, limiting or eliminating a potential Service Life Extension Program.

5.   Can the purchase of a Boeing 777F be funded with fuel savings?

Yes, surprisingly the Boeing 777F can be purchased with fuel savings money alone. The flight hours for the C-17A for 2011 and 2012 are in Table 5 below:

Table 5: C-17A Flight Hours FY 2011 and FY 2012 (AMC/A9)

2011 C-17 Flight Hours (Actual)	220996
2012 C-17 Flight Hours (Actual)	202124
Assume 7.9 Duration Flight -- # Flights 2011	27974.17722
Assume 7.9 Duration Flight -- # Flights 2012	25585.31646

Based upon a 7.9 hour flight, current operations tempo shows the C-17A accomplishing between 25,285 and 27,974 7.9 flights per Fiscal Year in 2011 and 2012.

Savings is evaluated either on a flight by flight basis or by accomplishing the analysis on the basis of the C-17A Flying Hour Program. Utilizing a flight by flight approach, based on 7.9 hour duration, the savings are shown below in Table 6.

Table 6: Savings Per Flight if utilizing Boeing 777F based on 7.9 hour flight at "Normal" Weight

Cost of Fuel	Savings Per Flight (7.9 hr)
2.80	$22,150.83
2.85	$22,546.38
2.90	$22,941.93
2.95	$23,337.48
3.00	$23,733.03
3.05	$24,128.58
3.10	$24,524.13
3.15	$24,919.68
3.20	$25,315.23
3.25	$25,710.78
3.30	$26,106.33
3.35	$26,501.88
3.40	$26,897.43
3.45	$27,292.98
3.50	$27,688.53
3.55	$28,084.08
3.60	$28,479.64
3.65	$28,875.19
3.70	$29,270.74
3.73	$29,508.07
3.75	$29,666.29
3.80	$30,061.84
3.85	$30,457.39
3.90	$30,852.94
3.95	$31,248.49
4.00	$31,644.04
4.05	$32,039.59
4.10	$32,435.14
4.15	$32,830.69
4.20	$33,226.24
4.25	$33,621.79
4.30	$34,017.34
4.35	$34,412.89
4.40	$34,808.44
4.45	$35,203.99
4.50	$35,599.54
4.55	$35,995.09
4.60	$36,390.64
4.65	$36,786.20
4.70	$37,181.75
4.75	$37,577.30
4.80	$37,972.85
4.85	$38,368.40
4.90	$38,763.95
4.95	$39,159.50
5.00	$39,555.05

The next advantage that saves money with regards to fuel is the sheer fact the Boeing 777F flies faster than the C-17A. The Boeing 777F can accomplish the same mission in .88 hours less which equates to 11216.216 pounds of fuel in savings per flight. Taking advantage of the faster flying Boeing 777F equates to savings in comparison to the C-17A (Table 7).

Table 7: Savings per flight based upon Boeing 777F flight duration for 7.9 hour C-17A equivalent flight

Cost of Fuel	Savings for faster flight	Total Savings
2.80	$4,687.37	$26,838.20
2.85	$4,771.08	$27,317.45
2.90	$4,854.78	$27,796.71
2.95	$4,938.48	$28,275.96
3.00	$5,022.19	$28,755.22
3.05	$5,105.89	$29,234.47
3.10	$5,189.59	$29,713.72
3.15	$5,273.30	$30,192.98
3.20	$5,357.00	$30,672.23
3.25	$5,440.70	$31,151.48
3.30	$5,524.40	$31,630.74
3.35	$5,608.11	$32,109.99
3.40	$5,691.81	$32,589.24
3.45	$5,775.51	$33,068.50
3.50	$5,859.22	$33,547.75
3.55	$5,942.92	$34,027.01
3.60	$6,026.62	$34,506.26
3.65	$6,110.33	$34,985.51
3.70	$6,194.03	$35,464.77
3.73	$6,244.25	$35,752.32
3.75	$6,277.73	$35,944.02
3.80	$6,361.44	$36,423.27
3.85	$6,445.14	$36,902.53
3.90	$6,528.84	$37,381.78
3.95	$6,612.55	$37,861.03
4.00	$6,696.25	$38,340.29
4.05	$6,779.95	$38,819.54
4.10	$6,863.65	$39,298.79
4.15	$6,947.36	$39,778.05
4.20	$7,031.06	$40,257.30
4.25	$7,114.76	$40,736.56
4.30	$7,198.47	$41,215.81
4.35	$7,282.17	$41,695.06
4.40	$7,365.87	$42,174.32
4.45	$7,449.58	$42,653.57
4.50	$7,533.28	$43,132.82
4.55	$7,616.98	$43,612.08
4.60	$7,700.69	$44,091.33
4.65	$7,784.39	$44,570.58
4.70	$7,868.09	$45,049.84
4.75	$7,951.79	$45,529.09
4.80	$8,035.50	$46,008.34
4.85	$8,119.20	$46,487.60
4.90	$8,202.90	$46,966.85
4.95	$8,286.61	$47,446.11
5.00	$8,370.31	$47,925.36

The other approach for evaluating savings based on fuel burn is to evaluate the C-17A Flying Hour program in relation to the Boeing 777F performance.

According to Boeing.com, the current "off the street" purchase price for a Boeing 777F is $295.7M per aircraft. Using this number, as the most conservative price, was then used to determine how many Boeing 777F per year could be "paid off" by accounting for the projected fuel savings of the aircraft. This calculation is accomplished utilizing 100% of the hours for the C-17A. This is not realistic, but can easily be adapted based on how many projected hours will accomplish only palletized cargo movements. The number of aircraft that can be purchased based on fuel savings alone, and the corresponding number of flights, assuming 7.9 hour duration, is shown in Table 8. This calculation was accomplished using the 2011 FY Flight Hours (Actual Flown) of 220,996 hours and a purchase price of $295.7M per Boeing 777F aircraft.

Table 8: Number of flights required to pay off one Boeing 777F and number of aircraft which can be paid off using fuel savings based on 100% of 2011 C-17A Flight Hours

Cost of Fuel	# Flights to "purchase" 1-777F	# of Aircraft Purchase
2.80	13349.39	2.10
2.85	13115.19	2.13
2.90	12889.06	2.17
2.95	12670.61	2.21
3.00	12459.43	2.25
3.05	12255.18	2.28
3.10	12057.51	2.32
3.15	11866.12	2.36
3.20	11680.71	2.39
3.25	11501.01	2.43
3.30	11326.75	2.47
3.35	11157.70	2.51
3.40	10993.61	2.54
3.45	10834.29	2.58
3.50	10679.51	2.62
3.55	10529.10	2.66
3.60	10382.86	2.69
3.65	10240.63	2.73
3.70	10102.24	2.77
3.73	10020.99	2.79
3.75	9967.54	2.81
3.80	9836.39	2.84
3.85	9708.65	2.88
3.90	9584.18	2.92
3.95	9462.86	2.96
4.00	9344.57	2.99
4.05	9229.21	3.03
4.10	9116.66	3.07
4.15	9006.82	3.11
4.20	8899.59	3.14
4.25	8794.89	3.18
4.30	8692.63	3.22
4.35	8592.71	3.26
4.40	8495.07	3.29
4.45	8399.62	3.33
4.50	8306.29	3.37
4.55	8215.01	3.41
4.60	8125.71	3.44
4.65	8038.34	3.48
4.70	7952.83	3.52
4.75	7869.11	3.55
4.80	7787.14	3.59
4.85	7706.86	3.63
4.90	7628.22	3.67
4.95	7551.17	3.70
5.00	7475.66	3.74

Table 9 shows the flights required to pay off a Boeing 777F and the total number of aircraft can be paid off, utilizing the same parameters as above, but including the added savings from the Boeing 777F flying faster than the C-17A.

Table 9: Number of flights required to pay off one Boeing 777F and number of aircraft which can be paid off using fuel savings based on 100% of 2011 C-17A Flight Hours including savings from Boeing 777F faster flying speed

Cost of Fuel	# Flights to "purchase" 1-777F	# of Aircraft Purchase
2.80	11017.88	2.54
2.85	10824.58	2.58
2.90	10637.95	2.63
2.95	10457.65	2.67
3.00	10283.35	2.72
3.05	10114.77	2.77
3.10	9951.63	2.81
3.15	9793.67	2.86
3.20	9640.64	2.90
3.25	9492.32	2.95
3.30	9348.50	2.99
3.35	9208.97	3.04
3.40	9073.55	3.08
3.45	8942.05	3.13
3.50	8814.30	3.17
3.55	8690.16	3.22
3.60	8569.46	3.26
3.65	8452.07	3.31
3.70	8337.85	3.36
3.73	8270.79	3.38
3.75	8226.68	3.40
3.80	8118.44	3.45
3.85	8013.00	3.49
3.90	7910.27	3.54
3.95	7810.14	3.58
4.00	7712.51	3.63
4.05	7617.30	3.67
4.10	7524.40	3.72
4.15	7433.75	3.76
4.20	7345.25	3.81
4.25	7258.84	3.85
4.30	7174.43	3.90
4.35	7091.97	3.94
4.40	7011.38	3.99
4.45	6932.60	4.04
4.50	6855.57	4.08
4.55	6780.23	4.13
4.60	6706.53	4.17
4.65	6634.42	4.22
4.70	6563.84	4.26
4.75	6494.75	4.31
4.80	6427.09	4.35
4.85	6360.84	4.40
4.90	6295.93	4.44
4.95	6232.33	4.49
5.00	6170.01	4.53

At the current fuel price of $3.73 per gallon of JP-8, if the Boeing 777F were utilized instead of the C-17A at the "normal" cargo weight, there is a $29,508.07 savings per flight just in fuel costs, based on 7.9 hour flight duration. The Boeing 777F accomplishes the same 7.9 hour flight that a C-17A accomplishes in .88 less flight hour. This translates into more fuels savings. Taking these savings into account, utilizing the Boeing 777F instead of the C-17A will save $35,752.32 per 7.9 hour C-17A equivalent flight. In all flight hours from the C-17A in FY 2011, were utilized by the Boeing 777F, then at $3.73 per gallon JP-8, the Air Force could purchase 2.73 Boeing 777F aircraft a year purely in fuel savings. Add in the fact that for every 7.9 hours flown by a C-17A, a Boeing 777F takes 7.02 hours to fly that same distance; thus, fuel is saved. The adjusted fuel savings allows for the Air Force to purchase 3.38 Boeing 777F aircraft a year purely based upon fuel savings.

Summary

It is clear from the analysis that the Boeing 777F is a more efficient and effective aircraft than the C-17A, when evaluated on palletized cargo airlift. The Boeing 777F is the right tool for oceanic palletized airlift when compared to the C-17A, especially when fuel burn is the primary consideration.

V. Conclusions and Recommendations

Chapter Overview

This chapter examines the basic conclusions about the research as well as managerial recommendations and areas for further research.

Conclusions of Research

It can be concluded from the research that the Boeing 777F is better suited to accomplish palletized cargo movement in direct comparison to the C-17A. Not only is the Boeing 777F a more effective aircraft, but it is also a more efficient than the C-17. Regardless of fuel price evaluated, from $2.80 to $5.00 per gallon of JP-8, the Boeing 777F is a more efficient aircraft. With the Boeing 777F carrying the same "normal" cargo weight as the C-17A, the Boeing 777F is more efficient.

Significance of Research

The research shows that using the wrong tool or wrong aircraft for the job impacts both efficiency and effectiveness. The Air Force must provide the best, most efficient and effective airlift for their customers; otherwise, the Air Force runs the risk of "over-pricing" themselves from the opportunity to move cargo. Additionally, for the Air Force, the bottom-line is national security. Not only is the Air Force responsible for aiding the nation in becoming less dependent on foreign oil, but they are also responsible for using the tools given to them in the most efficient and effective manner possible. Potential exists to extend the life cycle of the precious commodity known as the C-17A. If the Air

69

Force over-utilizes the C-17A, the operations that depend on its awesome capabilities are at risk.

Recommendations for Action

The Air Force is currently in an economic situation where they cannot afford to operate in accordance to its past: effectiveness cannot be the primary goal. Effectiveness is for instantaneous results and that is required of a military force; however E^2 must be utilized for training and sustainment operations. The Boeing 777F is an appropriate consideration for the Air Force based on this research.

Recommendations for Future Research

There are several recommendations for further research. First, it is recommended that the Air Force determines a fully burdened cost for the C-17, utilizing the "iceberg" approach in Figure 23, using it as a basic example, not all-inclusive.

In addition to evaluating the fully-burdened cost of the C-17A identify the true cost of flying the aircraft (and every aircraft in the AF inventory). Also, future research should investigate how the Air Force purchases "off-the-shelf" aircraft and aircraft parts potentially evaluating if the Air Force could combine purchases with civilian companies in order to bring costs per unit down. As an example, if the Air Force were to purchase Boeing 777F aircraft, they should consider combining their purchasing power with civilian companies like the airlines (both cargo and passenger) to purchase one big order.

This provides the best purchase option for all of the customers and provides for a strong order for Boeing, eliminating some of the uncertainty in government purchases. Additionally, this approach allows for the Air Force to purchase aircraft on a year by year basis at a better per unit cost: minimum price with maximum flexibility. In addition to researching the combined civilian and military purchasing power, the Air Force also needs to research if the C-17A is based appropriately.

Now that the Air Force has a plethora of C-17A's why are more C-17A's not stationed overseas in places like Germany, Italy, Japan and Guam. This re-basing would minimize the amount of long-haul oceanic palletized cargo movement accomplished by the C-17A. This must be approached from a life-cycle preservation approach.

Next, if purchasing the Boeing 777F is not an option the Air Force should consider a combination of "dry-lease" and Aircraft Crew Maintenance Insurance leases to accomplish the continuous palletized cargo movements. This allows for access to aircraft, but the burden of owning the aircraft does not fall on the Air Force.

Additionally, research needs to be accomplished to see what percentage of C-17A flying is dedicated to palletized movement. Also, the C-17A program needs to be evaluated to determine where in the overall life-cycle the aircraft program is established. In sync with the life cycle analysis, the C-17A flying hour program should be re-evaluated to determine what flying hours are required to accomplish the mission the aircraft was designed primarily to accomplish. All of the suggestions for research have one goal in mind, E^2.

The bottom line approach to our national security must be approached in an E^2

approach. If the Air Force does not seek efficiency to affect the monetary bottom line, then the ability to be effective will be diminished. Pure effectiveness is meant for instantaneous actions or operations, E^2 should be used for everything else from training to sustainment operations.

Summary

The Boeing 777F increases the security of the United States. Purchasing the Boeing 777F increases national security by decreasing the amount of fuel used in flight operations, and allows for potential life cycle extension of the highly utilized C-17A. Amazingly, fuel saved by not flying the C-17A actually allows for purchasing the Boeing 777F. The country is in a difficult financial situation, as is the Air Force. E^2 is the beginning of the solution equation.

Bibliography

Battershell, A. Lee. *The DOD C-17 versus the Boeing 777 A Comparison of Acquisition and Development.* Washington D.C.: U.S. Government Printing Office, 1999.

Boeing. "Jet Prices." Excerpt from website. n. pag. http://www.boeing.com/boeing/commercial/prices. 26 March 2013.

Bowers, Peter M. *Boeing Aircraft since 1916.* Oxford: Putnam Aeronautical books, 1993.

Conaton, Erin C., Undersecretary of the Air Force. "A New Culture: Energy as an Operations Enabler." Keynote Address to the USAF Energy Forum III. Washington, D.C. 27 May 2010.

Department of the Air Force. *Air Mobility Planning Factors.* Air Force Pamphlet 10-1403. Washington: HQ USAF, 12 December 2011.

Government Accountability Office. *Defense Transportation: Air Mobility Command Needs to Collect and Analyze Better Data to Assess Aircraft Utilization.* GAO-05-819. Washington: GPO, 2005.

Government Accountability Office. *Defense Transportation: Additional Information Is Needed for DOD's Mobility Capabilities and Requirements Study 2016 to Fully Address All of Its Study Objectives.* GAO-11-82R. Washington: GPO, 2010.

Jackson, Robert. *The Berlin Airlift.* Wellingborough: Patrick Stephens, 1988.

Kennedy, Betty R. *Globemaster III Acquiring the C-17.* Air Mobility Command: Scott Air Force Base, 2004.

Knight, William. *Strategic Airlift Modernization: Analysis of C-5 Modernization and C-17 Acquisition Issues.* Congressional Research Service: Washington D.C., 2008.

Martin, Bricker. Director, Military Operations, Atlas Airlines. Scott Air Force Base, Illinois. Personal Correspondence. 29 April 2013.

Maybury, Mark T. Dr. "Energy Horizons: A Science and Technology Vision for Air Force Energy," *Air & Space Power Journal*, 2: 3-30 (March-April 2012).

Multinational Air Freight Company that Operates the Boeing 777F. 6 March 2013 and 21 March 2013.

Office of the Secretary of Defense. *Executive Summary: Mobility Capabilities and Requirements Study.* Washington: GPO, 2010.

Paulus, John. *C-17 Maximum Weight Computer Flight Plan.* Air Mobility Command Fuel Efficiency Office: Scott Air Force Base, 4 December 2012.

Pearcy, Arthur. *Berlin Airlift.* Shrewsbury: Airlife Publishing, 1997.

Robertson, John D. Capabilities IPT, Wright Patterson AFB, Ohio. Personal Correspondence. 25 March 2013.

Wikipedia. "C-1 Douglas Aircraft" Excerpt from website. n. pag. http://en.wikipedia.org/wiki/Douglas_C-1. 1 Feb 2013.

www.ingramcontent.com/pod-product-compliance
Lightning Source LLC
Chambersburg PA
CBHW081847280526
45789CB00007B/2599